Springer Texts in Social Sciences

This textbook series delivers high-quality instructional content for graduates and advanced graduates in the social sciences. It comprises self-contained edited or authored books with comprehensive international coverage that are suitable for class as well as for individual self-study and professional development. The series covers core concepts, key methodological approaches, and important issues within key social science disciplines and also across these disciplines. All texts are authored by established experts in their fields and offer a solid methodological background, accompanied by pedagogical materials to serve students, such as practical examples, exercises, case studies etc. Textbooks published in this series are aimed at graduate and advanced graduate students, but are also valuable to early career and established researchers as important resources for their education, knowledge and teaching.

The books in this series may come under, but are not limited to, these fields:

-- Sociology
-- Anthropology
-- Population studies
-- Migration studies
-- Quality of life and wellbeing research

Arthur Asa Berger

Everyday Life in the Postmodern World

An Introduction to Cultural Studies

Arthur Asa Berger
Broadcast & Electronic Communication Arts Department
San Francisco State University
San Francisco, CA, USA

ISSN 2730-6135　　　　　　　ISSN 2730-6143　(electronic)
Springer Texts in Social Sciences
ISBN 978-3-031-07925-2　　　ISBN 978-3-031-07926-9　(eBook)
https://doi.org/10.1007/978-3-031-07926-9

© The Editor(s) (if applicable) and The Author(s), under exclusive licence to Springer Nature Switzerland AG 2022
This work is subject to copyright. All rights are solely and exclusively licensed by the Publisher, whether the whole or part of the material is concerned, specifically the rights of translation, reprinting, reuse of illustrations, recitation, broadcasting, reproduction on microfilms or in any other physical way, and transmission or information storage and retrieval, electronic adaptation, computer software, or by similar or dissimilar methodology now known or hereafter developed.
The use of general descriptive names, registered names, trademarks, service marks, etc. in this publication does not imply, even in the absence of a specific statement, that such names are exempt from the relevant protective laws and regulations and therefore free for general use.
The publisher, the authors, and the editors are safe to assume that the advice and information in this book are believed to be true and accurate at the date of publication. Neither the publisher nor the authors or the editors give a warranty, expressed or implied, with respect to the material contained herein or for any errors or omissions that may have been made. The publisher remains neutral with regard to jurisdictional claims in published maps and institutional affiliations.

This Springer imprint is published by the registered company Springer Nature Switzerland AG.
The registered company address is: Gewerbestrasse 11, 6330 Cham, Switzerland

For Wendy and Ivan Levison

Acknowledgments

I would like to thank all the writers, thinkers, theorists, scholars, philosophers, and others from whom I have quoted and whose ideas have influenced my thinking. I would also like to express my appreciation for the encouragement of my editor, Shinjini Chaterjee, and the production staff at Springer for their help in publishing this book.

Contents

Part I Cultural Studies and Everyday Life	1
1 Introduction	3
Media, Popular Culture, and Everyday Life	5
The Title: Everyday Life in the Postmodern World	9
Modernism and Postmodernism	11
References	14
2 Notes on American National Character	15
Literacy Rate	16
A Note on American National Character	17
Clotaire Rapaille on The Culture Code *(Fig. 2.2)*	18
Geoffrey Gorer on How Cultures Maintain Themselves	21
The Complexities of Everyday Life	21
References	23
3 A Cultural Studies Analysis of Everyday Life	25
Semiotic Theory and Everyday Life	27
Reading People	28
Ferdinand de Saussure (Fig. 3.1)	28
Charles Sanders Peirce (Fig. 3.2)	30
Key Statements by Semiotic Theorists	32
The Marxist Analysis of Everyday Life	34
Key Statements by Marxist Theorists	36
Psychoanalytic Theory and Everyday Life	39
Freud's Topographic Hypothesis	39
Freud's Structural Hypothesis	41
Key Statements by Psychoanalytic Theorists	42

      Basic Elements of Psychoanalysis   42
      Sociological Theory   44
      Key Statements by Sociological Theorists   50
   References   55

4 Media and Everyday Life   57
   Timeline on the Internet   59
   Time Spent with Traditional vs Digital Media   61
   Focal Points for the Study of Media   63
   Case Study: Metaphor and "All in the Game"   64
   Media Effects   66
   Social Media: Revelations about Facebook's Impact   67
   Social Media: Facebook and the Net Effect   68
   Social Media: The Internet and Depression   68
   Uses and Gratifications Theory: A Different Approach to Media Research   69
   Genres and the Media   70
   A Case Study: Gratifications from Romance Novels   72
   The Importance of Narratives   73
   Grid-Group Theory: Media Preferences for Specific Texts   74
   Marshall McLuhan on Media   78
   Statistics on Interest in the Media   80
   Googling Media   80
   Amazon Books on Media   80
   References   81

5 The Postmodern Sacred in America   83
   Case Study 1: Football as a Sacred Ritual   93
   Case Study 2: Running for President   97
   Case Study 3: Selling and the Sacred   100
   Case Study 4: Pilgrims and Cruise Passengers   105
   Case Study 5: The Crying of Lot 49   109
   References   114

Part II   My Contributions to the Study of Everyday Life   115

6 My Contributions to Analyzing Everyday Life and Postmodernism: From a Cultural Studies Perspective   117
   McDonald's "Evangelical" Hamburgers   119
      Bloom's Morning: Coffee, Comforters, and the Secret Meaning of Everyday Life   120
      Postmortem for a Postmodernist   121

The Amazon Echo Dot	122
"Pac-Man"	124
Is Bali Postmodern?	125
My Name Is Sherlock Holmes: Sherlock Holmes is Introduced to Cultural Theory	126
Three Tropes on Trump (Fig. 6.6)	128
Erich Fromm on Marxism and Psychoanalysis	132
Learning from Las Vegas	133
References	134

7 **An Ethnographic Case Study: My Everyday Life During the Pandemic** — 137
   References — 146

8 **Coda** — 147
   References — 153

Glossary — 155

References — 163

About the Author

Arthur Asa Berger is professor emeritus of Broadcast and Electronic Communication Arts at San Francisco State University, where he taught between 1965 and 2003. He graduated in 1954 from the University of Massachusetts, where he majored in literature and philosophy. He received an MA degree in journalism and creative writing from the University of Iowa in 1956. He was drafted shortly after graduating from Iowa and served in the US Army in the Military District of Washington in Washington DC, where he was a feature writer and speechwriter in the District's Public Information Office. He also wrote about high school sports for *The Washington Post* on weekend evenings while in the army.

Berger spent a year touring Europe after he got out of the Army and then went to the University of Minnesota, where he received a Ph.D. in American Studies in 1965. He wrote his dissertation on the comic strip *Li'l Abner*. In 1963-64, he had a Fulbright to Italy and taught at the University of Milan. He spent a year as a visiting professor at the Annenberg School for Communication at the University of Southern California in Los Angeles in 1984 and two months in the fall of 2007 as a visiting professor at the School of Hotel and Tourism in Hong Kong Polytechnic University. He spent a month lecturing at Jinan University in Guangzhou and ten days lecturing at Tsinghua University in Beijing in the spring of 2009.

He is the author of more than one hundred articles published in the USA and abroad, numerous book reviews, and more than 80 books on the mass media, popular culture, humor, tourism, and everyday life. Among his books are *Bloom's Morning; The Academic Writer's Toolkit: A User's Manual; Media Analysis Technique; Seeing is Believing: An Introduction to Visual Communication; Ads, Fads And Consumer Culture; The Art of Comedy Writing;* and *Shop 'Til You Drop: Consumer Behavior and American Culture.* Berger is also an artist and has illustrated many of his books.

He has also written many comic academic mysteries such as *Postmortem for a Postmodernist, Mistake in Identity, The Mass Comm Murders: Five Media Theorists Self-Destruct,* and *Durkheim is Dead: Sherlock Holmes is Introduced to Sociological Theory.* His books have been translated into German, Italian, Russian, Arabic, Swedish, Korean, Turkish, and Chinese, and he has lectured in more than a dozen countries in the course of his career.

Berger is married, has two children and four grandchildren, and lives in Mill Valley, California. He enjoys travel and listening to classical music. He can be reached by e-mail at arthurasaberger@gmail.com.

List of Figures

Fig. 1.1	Robert Musil	4
Fig. 1.2	Henri Lefebvre	6
Fig. 1.3	Pastiche. By the Author	8
Fig. 1.4	Cover of *Everyday Life in the Modern World*	8
Fig. 1.5	Jean-François Lyotard	11
Fig. 1.6	Daily Calendar	14
Fig. 2.1	American flag	17
Fig. 2.2	Clotaire Rapaille	19
Fig. 2.3	Geoffrey Gorer	20
Fig. 3.1	Ferdinand de Saussure	29
Fig. 3.2	Charles Sanders Peirce	30
Fig. 3.3	Umberto Eco	32
Fig. 3.4	Karl Marx	34
Fig. 3.5	Roland Barthes	35
Fig. 3.6	Theodor W. Adorno	37
Fig. 3.7	*Bloom's Morning*	39
Fig. 3.8	Sigmund Freud	40
Fig. 3.9	Iceberg simile for the psyche	41
Fig. 3.10	Id, ego, superego in the mind	42
Fig. 3.11	Auguste Comte	45
Fig. 3.12	Emile Durkheim	45
Fig. 3.13	Pierre Bourdieu	46
Fig. 3.14	W. Lloyd Warner	47
Fig. 3.15	Max Weber	48
Fig. 3.16	Georg Simmel	51
Fig. 3.17	Michel de Certeau	54
Fig. 4.1	Focal points in studying media	64
Fig. 4.2	The Game of Love	64
Fig. 4.3	Marshall McLuhan	78
Fig. 5.1	Mircea Eliade	85
Fig. 5.2	Theseus Killing the Minotaur	86
Fig. 5.3	Jean Baudrillard	91
Fig. 5.4	Football stadium	93

Fig. 5.5	Football game. Photo by the Author from Television	94
Fig. 5.6	Washington monument	97
Fig. 5.7	Trump rally. Photo by the Author from Television Coverage	98
Fig. 5.8	Consume	100
Fig. 5.9	John Calvin	101
Fig. 5.10	Cathedral in Barcelona	103
Fig. 5.11	Jonathan Edwards	105
Fig. 5.12	Travel photos of Arthur Asa Berger	105
Fig. 5.13	*The Star Princess*. Photo by the Author	107
Fig. 5.14	Prime Rib Dinner on the *Star Princess*. Photo by the Author	107
Fig. 5.15	Mikhail Bakhtin	108
Fig. 6.1	McDonald's. Photo by the author	119
Fig. 6.2	*Postmortem for a Postmodernist* cover	121
Fig. 6.3	The Amazon Echo Dot	123
Fig. 6.4	Bali dance scene	125
Fig. 6.5	Sherlock Holmes	126
Fig. 6.6	Trump balloon	128
Fig. 6.7	Erich Fromm	131
Fig. 7.1	Three-quart Instant Pot	140
Fig. 7.2	Three Tropes on Trump	141
Fig. 7.3	Oatmeal breakfast	141
Fig. 7.4	Journal page	142
Fig. 7.5	*The Golden Triangle: An Ethno-Semiotic Tour of Present-Day India*	143
Fig. 7.6	The Prisoner meets the first Number Two	145
Fig. 7.7	Rover, The Killer Balloon, in *The Prisoner*	146
Fig. 7.8	The Coronavirus	146
Fig. 8.1	Journal page when the idea of writing a book came to me	149
Fig. 8.2	Journal page: Brainstorming on everyday life	150
Fig. 8.3	Cover of *Pop Culture*	151

LIST OF TABLES

Table 1.1	The quotidian and the modern	9
Table 1.2	Modernism and postmodernism contrasted	13
Table 3.1	Peirce's analysis of kinds of signs	31
Table 3.2	Id, ego, and superego applied to society	42
Table 4.1	Time spent with electronic media in 2013	61
Table 4.2	Time spent with traditional vs. digital media in US	62
Table 4.3	Minutes spent per person per medium	63
Table 4.4	Formulas in popular literature genres	71
Table 4.5	Lifestyle group boundaries and rules	75
Table 4.6	Lifestyles and media preferences	77
Table 4.7	McLuhan on electronic and print media	79
Table 4.8	McLuhan on hot and cool media	80
Table 5.1	Modernism and postmodernism compared	89
Table 5.2	Results on Google for modernism and postmodernism searches	90
Table 5.3	The sacred and the profane	92
Table 5.4	Football as a functional alternative to religion	95
Table 5.5	Department store as functional alternative to cathedral	104
Table 5.6	Pilgrimage and regular travel compared	106
Table 8.1	Average time spent per day with major media by US adults	148

PART I

Cultural Studies and Everyday Life

CHAPTER 1

Introduction

Chapter Objectives This chapter points out that the book will offer primers on the four basic methodologies of cultural studies—semiotic theory, psychoanalytic theory, Marxist theory, and sociological theory and will offer examples of how these disciplines can be used in cultural studies works. It also will offer numerous quotations from the works of important writers and thinkers so readers can see not only what was said but how it was said. The book was inspired by the French sociologist Henri Lefebvre's *Everyday Life in the Modern World* and focuses on everyday life in the postmodern world. Postmodernism is a subject about which there is considerable controversy. The writings of Jean-Francois Lyotard on postmodernism are discussed along with definitions of the terms quotidian and everyday. There is a chart comparing the quotidian and the modern and another chart on modernism and postmodernism. It concludes with a discussion of metaphor and the role of metaphor in our thinking, pointing out that metaphor is an essential part of our everyday thought.

Keywords Semiotics • Psychoanalytic theory • Marxist theory • Sociological theory • Modernism • Postmodernism

https://en.wikipedia.org/wiki/Pierre_Bourdieu

https://en.wikipedia.org/wiki/Influence_of_mass_media

> At this moment he wished to be a man without qualities. But this is probably not so different from what other people sometimes feel too. After all, by the time they have reached the middle of their life's journey few people remember how they have managed to arrive at themselves, at their amusements, their point of view, their wife, character, occupation and successes, but they cannot help feeling that not much is likely to change any more. It might even be asserted that they have been cheated, for one can nowhere discover any sufficient reason for everything's having come about as it has. It might just as well have turned out differently. The events of people's lives have, after all, only to the least degree originated in them, having generally depended on all sorts of circumstances such as the moods, the life or death of quite different people, and have, as it were, only at the given point of time come hurrying towards them.... Something has had its way with them like a flypaper with a fly; it has caught them fast, here catching a little hair, there hampering their movements, and has gradually enveloped them, until they lie, buried under a thick coating that has only the remotest resemblance to their original shape.

Robert Musil, *The Man Without Qualities* (1965) (Fig. 1.1)

Fig. 1.1 Robert Musil

> Many everyday practices (talking, reading, moving about, shopping, cooking, etc.) are tactical in character. And so are, more generally, many "ways of operating": victories of the "weak" over the "strong" (whether the strength be that of powerful people or the violence of things or of an imposed order, etc.) clever tricks, knowing how to get away with things, "hunter's cunning," maneuvers, polymorphic simulations, joyful discoveries poetic as well as warlike.

> Michel de Certeau. *The Practice of Everyday Life*. (1984, p. 166)

For as long as I can remember, I've been writing about everyday life and popular culture from a cultural studies perspective. My first book was published in 1970. It was based on my Ph.D. dissertation on *Li'l Abner*, a comic strip that was part of the everyday life media diet for millions of Americans for many decades. And any number of my books on media and popular culture had everyday life as part of their titles.

Media, Popular Culture, and Everyday Life

For example, one of my most recent books was titled *Applied Discourse Analysis: Popular Culture, Media, and Everyday Life* (2016, Palgrave). In 2003, I published a book, *The Agent in the Agency: Media, Popular Culture, and Everyday Life in America*, (2003, Hampton Press) which also had everyday life on the subtitle.

I also wrote a book, *Perspectives on Everyday Life: A Cross Disciplinary Analysis* (Palgrave, 2018), about everyday life that deals with theories about everyday life and American material culture and popular culture. It has chapters on books such as Henri Lefebvre's *Everyday Life in the Modern World*, Michel de Certeau's *The Practice of Everyday Life*, Fernand Braudel's *The Structures of Everyday Life*, Sigmund Freud's *Psychopathology and Everyday Life*, and Milton Sapirstein's *The Paradoxes of Everyday Life*.

The title of this book, *Everyday Life in the Postmodern World*, is a play on Lefebvre's classic, *Everyday Life in the Modern World*, a book that has influenced my thinking in many ways. Lefebvre published his book in France in 1968, just when the modern world was becoming the postmodern world.

Fig. 1.2 Henri Lefebvre

The English version of Lefebvre's book was published by Harper in 1971. So my book will be different from Lefebvre's in that I will be dealing with the postmodern world—a subject that I've dealt with in several books, such as *The Portable Postmodernist* (2003, AltaMira Press), and my academic murder mystery, *Postmortem for a Postmodernist* (1997, AltaMira Press), and other articles and books (Fig. 1.2).

You can see from this introduction that I've been writing about media, popular culture, everyday life, and postmodernism from a cultural studies perspective for many years. In this book, I will do a few things:

1. I will provide primers about the four most important disciplines involved in the field of cultural studies: semiotics, psychoanalytic theory, Marxism, and sociological theory. These primers offer a theoretical base that my readers can use to make their own analyses of popular culture, everyday life, and anything else that might be of interest to them. Learning methodologies empower people and my teaching always involved helping my students learn the most important disciplinary techniques of analysis.
2. In the second part of the book, I will offer examples of the way I have used a cultural studies approach to analyze many different aspects of popular culture, postmodernism, and everyday life. That way, my readers will be able to see how a cultural studies approach can be applied to many different aspects of these topics. Many of my books have a common

structure: a theoretical section and then an applications section in which my readers can see how the theories can be used. These theories stay with people. I recall being in a supermarket and meeting a student of mine from 30 years ago who said to me, "You know that semiotics you taught us? It's still with me."
3. I will offer numerous quotations from important thinkers in various fields who have interesting things to say about many topics. *I do this so my readers can see what the thinkers and theorists I quote from had to say about some topic I'm writing about and how they said it.* You can think about these quotations as similar to evidence in a trial and I use my thinkers to support my case. None of the quotations in the book are longer than 350 words except those from books for which I have the copyright.

    I've added short quotations from my thinkers and theorists in different sections of the book in what you might think of as a micro anthology of key statements. This means that readers of this book will have read writings by thinkers such as Henri Lefebvre, Ferdinand de Saussure, Charles Sanders Peirce, Sigmund Freud, Karl Marx, Vladimir Lenin, Jean Baudrillard, Pierre Bourdieu, M.M. Bakhtin, and many others. And I've added a chapter with many excerpts from my writings on everyday life, popular culture, and postmodernism. You can think of this feature as a micro-reader with key statements by seminal thinkers.
4. Since we live in a postmodern world (though some would say we now live in a post-postmodern world), I discuss postmodernism in some detail. It is generally held that postmodernism became a cultural dominant in the sixties. In the best postmodern tradition, this book can be considered a pastiche (the dominant postmodern art form) in that it incorporates elements from texts by many authors and an example of intertextuality—a concept based on the Russian communications theorist Bakhtin's notion that all texts are tied to previous texts just as all conversations are tied to all previous and future conversations (Fig. 1.3).

I try to write in an accessible, conversational style to make my books as "reader-friendly" as possible. But the content of the book, you will find, is very high level with discussions of the ideas of some of our greatest thinkers. I'd like to think that readers of this book, thanks to the discussions and the quotations, will end up having what I think of as a liberal education.

I've also illustrated the book with many of my drawings and my photographs to give the book more visual appeal. I think the look of a book is important (Fig. 1.4).

On the cover of Lefebvre's book, we see a bottle of milk, a glass of milk, and a bowl of cereal on a kitchen table and, in the window, an atomic bomb going off. We have two items that show the extremes of everyday life: the mundane quotidian and the world-changing.

Fig. 1.3 Pastiche. By the Author

Fig. 1.4 Cover of *Everyday Life in the Modern World*

The Title: Everyday Life in the Postmodern World

The Cambridge Dictionary lists some synonyms for quotidian or everyday:

Everyday, Mundane, Unremarkable, Workaday
An Internet Source provides the etymology of the term:

> Etymology. From Anglo-Norman cotidian, cotidien, Middle French cotidian, cotidien, and their source, Latin cottīdiānus, quōtīdiānus ("happening every day"), from adverb cottīdiē, quōtīdiē ("every day, daily"), from an unattested adjective derived from quote ("how many") + locative form of diēs ("day").

Lefebvre describes the quotidian as follows (1971, p. 24):

> The quotidian is what is humble and solid, what is taken from granted and thus that of which all the parts follow each other in such a regular, unvarying succession that those concerned have no call to question their sequence; thus it is undated and (apparently) insignificant; though it occupies and preoccupies it is practically untellable.

He contrasts this with the modern (1971, p. 24):

> This word stands for what is novel, brilliant, paradoxical, and bears the imprint of technicality and worldliness; it is (apparently) daring and transitory, proclaims its initiative is acclaimed for it; it is art and aestheticism....

We can see the differences between the quotidian or everyday and the modern in Table 1.1 that follows (my construction):

I use oppositions because binary oppositions are the main instrument by which we make sense of concepts. In his book *Semiotics: The Basics* 3rd edition,

Table 1.1 The quotidian and the modern

Quotidian	*Modern*
Humble	Elevated
Taken for granted	Discerned
Unvarying	Changeable
Undated	Dated
Everyday	Occasional
Routine	Novel
Fixed	Chanced
Mundane	Remarkable
No style	Fashionable
Unexamined	Interpreted
Taken for granted	Irregular
Signifiers	Signified

Daniel Chandler provides some important insights relative to the problems binary oppositions cause (2017, p. 107):

> Binarism is rightly criticized when it leads to negative stereotyping and when it is uncritically accepted as "the real"—as in common-sense assumptions that supposedly either/or oppositions, such as male and female, or heterosexual and homosexual, exhaust the possibilities of the domains they purport to encompass....Conceptual binaries have been prominent throughout history in political rhetoric and propaganda—and have indeed been used to instigate countless wars. However, the oppositions (or whatever kind) which we employ in our cultural practices help to generate order out of the dynamic complexity of experience. Our entire system of values is built upon oppositions, which exist within sign systems rather than in the world.

Chandler reminds us to be careful about assuming that bipolar oppositions are adequate to deal with the complexities of human experience and culture, even though we use them to make sense of many things in our everyday lives.

Ferdinand de Saussure, one of the founding fathers of semiotics, the science of signs, tells us that in language there are only differences. So we make sense of words by recognizing their opposites. It sounds crazy, but words take their meaning by being the opposite of other words. Saussure explained that concepts only have meaning because of their relationships with other concepts. Their basic relationship is oppositional. As he explained: (1966, p. 120) "In language, there are only differences." He added (1966, p. 117):

> Concepts are purely differential and defined not by their positive content but negatively by their relations with the other terms of the system.

We find, then, that it is not the "content" of a concept that determines its meaning, but "relations" among concepts in some kind of a system, which explains why he wrote that (1966, pp. 117, 118):

> The most precise characteristic [of these concepts] is in being what the others are not. Signs function not through their intrinsic value but through their relative position.

This means that we determine the meaning of a concept by recognizing what it is not. We can see this readily enough in language, but it also holds for signs of all kinds. Nothing has meaning in itself! This explains why my chart is based on bipolar oppositions, for it is through oppositions in language that we make sense of the meaning of things.

Modernism and Postmodernism

We can also use a chart to distinguish between modernism and postmodernism. Roughly speaking, the ideas, beliefs, and values associated with modernism dominated American culture and society until around 1960, when there was a cultural mutation, and postmodernism became culturally dominant.

The term "modern" is derived from the fifth-century Latin word *modernus*, which was used to differentiate the pagan era from the Christian era. Bryan S. Turner argues in his book *Theories of Modernity and Postmodernity* that we can equate modernism with a rejection of history and with the notion of differentiation.

This means that postmodernism involves a kind of cultural de-differentiation. It turns out that postmodernism develops at the same time that consumer capitalism becomes dominant which explains why postmodernism is associated with consumer culture and mass consumption, which affects fashion and shapes everyone's lifestyles. As we might expect, postmodernism is intimately connected to the system it rejected and replaced—modernism (Fig. 1.5).

In the chart below I list many of the oppositions between modernism and postmodernism, some of which I will discuss later in the book. One of the most famous descriptions of postmodernism is found in Jean-François Lyotard's *The Postmodern Condition: A Report on Knowledge*. University of Minnesota Press. (1984, p. xxiv):

Fig. 1.5 Jean-François Lyotard

> Simplifying to the extreme, I define *postmodern* as incredulity toward metanarratives. This incredulity is undoubtedly a product of progress in the sciences: but that progress in turn presupposes it. To the obsolescence of the metanarrative apparatus of legitimation corresponds, most notably, the crisis of metaphysical philosophy and of the university institution which in the past relied on it. The narrative function is losing its functors, its great hero, its great dangers, its great voyages, its great goal.

Lyotard is calling attention to the rejection of metanarratives, the great systems of philosophy and thought that dominated life in modernism—a belief in progress, philosophy, rationality, logic, institutions, and the centered self. Steven Best and Douglas Kellner offer additional insights in their book *Postmodern Theory: Critical Interrogations* (1991, p. 19):

> Postmodern discourses thus denote new artistic, cultural, or theoretical perspectives which renounce modern discourses and practices. All of these "post" terms function as sequential markers, designating that which follows and comes after the modern. The discourse of postmodernism thus involves periodizing terms which describe a set of key changes in history, society, culture, and thought. The confusion involved in the discourse of the postmodern results from its usage in different fields and disciplines and the fact that most theorists and commentators on postmodern discourse provide definitions and conceptualizations that are frequently at odds with each other and usually inadequately theorized. Moreover, some theorists and commentators use the term postmodernism descriptively, to describe new phenomena, while others use it prescriptively, urging the adoption of new theoretical, cultural, and political discourses and practices.

Todd Gitlin, a sociologist, offers us a list of important postmodernist architects, artists, musicians, and writers in his article "Postmodernism Defined, At Last," published in *The New York Times* (Nov. 6, 1989):

A Postmodern Trope

> One postmodernist trope is the list, as if culture were a garage sale, so it is appropriate to evoke postmodernism by offering a list of examples, for better or worse: Michael Graves' Portland Building, Philip Johnson's AT&T, and hundreds of more or less skillful derivatives; Robert Rauschenberg's silkscreens, Warhol's multiple-image paintings, photo-realism, Larry Rivers' erasures and pseudo-pageantry, Sherrie Levine's photographs of "classic" photographs; Disneyland, Las Vegas, suburban strips, shopping malls, mirror-glass building facades, William Burroughs, Tom Wolfe, Donald Barthelme, Monty Python, Don DeLillo, Joe Isuzu "He's lying commercials, Philip Glass, *Star Wars,* Spalding Gray, David Hockney ("Surface is illusion, but so is depth"), Max Headroom, Twyla Tharp (choreographic Beach Boys and Frank Sinatra songs), Italo Calvino, *The Gospel of Colonus,* Robert Wilson, the Flying Karamazov Brothers, George Coates, the Kronos Quartet, Frederic Barthelme, MTV, *Miami Vice....*

Table 1.2 Modernism and postmodernism contrasted

Modernism	*Postmodernism*
Master narratives valued	Master narratives rejected
Belief in progress	Rejection of belief in progress
Hierarchy, centralized control	Subversion of hierarchy
European, Western	Global, multicultural
Detached	Participatory
Serious	Playful, ironic
High and low culture different	High and low culture the same
Stylistic purity	Stylistic eclecticism
Material	Semiotic
Harmonious	Discordant
Unified self	Fragmented self
Realism	The Pastiche
We can know reality	Illusions and hyperreality dominate
Production culture	Consumption culture
Businessmen, statesmen heroes	Celebrities, entertainers heroes

With these insights in mind, let us consider my chart in which I compare modernism and postmodernism in terms of their basic attributes (Table 1.2):

When making a table like this, you have to simplify things and sometimes I take minor liberties to find concepts that provide the correct oppositions. But charts are useful because they allow readers to see relationships very quickly and it is relationships that generate knowledge and understanding. As George Lakoff and Mark Johnson explain in *Metaphors We Live By* (1980, p. 3):

> The concepts that govern our thought are not just matters of the intellect. They also govern our everyday functioning, down to the most mundane details. Our concepts structure what we perceive, how we get around in the world, and how we relate to other people. Our conceptual system thus plays a central role in defining our everyday realities. If we are right in suggesting that our conceptual system is largely metaphorical, what we experience and what we do every day is very much a matter of metaphor.

Metaphors are figures of speech that shape our thinking. They are based on association and generally involve some version of the verb "to be" as in "My love *is* a red rose." A weaker form of metaphor, simile, uses "like" or "as" in comparing two things, as in "My love *is like* a red rose." People may not be aware of what they are doing but according to Lakoff and Johnson, the average person uses metaphors and similes many times a day in their speech (Fig. 1.6).

In this chapter, I have defined the terms "everyday" and a different way of saying the same thing, "quotidian," suggesting that they involve the ordinary and unexamined and routine aspects of our daily lives, and I've discussed modernism and postmodernism. I offered a chart comparing the quotidian and the modern and another chart comparing modernism and postmodernism.

Fig. 1.6 Daily Calendar

REFERENCES

Best, Steven, and Douglas Kellner. 1991. *Postmodern theory: Critical interrogations*. New York, NY: Guilford.
Chandler, Daniel. 2017. *Semiotics: The basics*. 3rd ed. London: Routledge.
de Certeau, Michel. 1984. *The practice of everyday life*. Berkeley, CA: University of California Press.
de Saussure, Ferdinand. 1966. *Course in general linguistics*. New York, NY: McGraw-Hill.
Todd Gitlin, "Postmodernism Defined at Last," *New York Times*. Also in the *Utne Reader*. July–August, 1989.
Lakoff, George, and Mark Johnson. 1980. *Metaphors we live by*. Chicago, IL: University of Chicago Press.
Lefebvre, Henri. 1971. *Everyday life in the modern world*. New York: Harper & Row.
Lyotard, Jean-François. 1984. *The postmodern condition: A report on knowledge*. Minneapolis: University of Minnesota Press.
Musil, Robert. 1965. *The man without qualities*. Vol. 1. New York, NY: Capricorn.

CHAPTER 2

Notes on American National Character

Chapter Objectives The focus in this chapter is upon American national character and factors affecting it. It offers a brief examination of literacy rates in America and suggests that 43 million Americans have low literacy rates which has an impact on American politics and society. An article by journalist David Brooks is quoted dealing with the idea of American exceptionalism which is how Americans tend to think about themselves. The ideas of a French psychoanalyst and marketing expert Clotaire Rapaille are discussed. He suggests that by the age of seven, children are imprinted with the things that matter most in a given society and this imprinting affects their behavior when older. This is followed by a discussion of the theories of Geoffrey Gorer, an English anthropologist, about the way cultures maintain themselves. The chapter concludes with a discussion of psychographic and demographic factors shaping everyday life such as age, gender, ethnicity, race, and religion.

Keywords Literacy • American exceptionalism • Imprinting • National character

> Nacirema culture is characterized by a highly developed market economy which has evolved in a rich natural habitat. While much of the people's time is devoted to economic pursuits, a large part of the fruits of these labors and a considerable portion of the day are spent in ritual activity. The focus of this activity is the human body, the appearance and health of which loom as a dominant concern in the ethos of the people. While such a concern is certainly not unusual, its ceremonial aspects and associated philosophy are unique.

> The fundamental belief underlying the whole system appears to be that the human body is ugly and that its natural tendency is to debility and disease. Incarcerated in such a body, man's only hope is to avert these characteristics through the use of ritual and ceremony. Every household has one or more shrines devoted to this purpose. The more powerful individuals in the society have several shrines in their houses and, in fact, the opulence of a house is often referred to in terms of the number of such ritual centers it possesses. Most houses are of wattle and daub construction, but the shrine rooms of the more wealthy are walled with stone. Poorer families imitate the rich by applying pottery plaques to their shrine walls.

> While each family has at least one such shrine, the rituals associated with it are not family ceremonies but are private and secret. The rites are normally only discussed with children, and then only during the period when they are being initiated into these mysteries. I was able, however, to establish sufficient [504 begins ->] rapport with the natives to examine these shrines and to have the rituals described to me.

> Horace Miner, *Body Ritual Among the Nacirema*. *American Anthropologist*, 1956, 58(3), 503–507

In this chapter, I start with some statistics on American literacy and then discuss national character and American character and culture (Fig. 2.1).

Literacy Rate

According to the National Center for Educational Statistics, many Americans possess low literacy skills:

> Four in five U.S. adults (79 percent) have English literacy skills sufficient to complete tasks that require comparing and contrasting information, paraphrasing, or making low-level inferences—literacy skills at level 2 or above in PIAAC (OECD, 2013). In contrast, one in five U.S. adults (21 percent) has difficulty completing these tasks (Fig. 1). This translates into 43.0 million U.S. adults who possess low literacy skills: 26.5 million at level 1 and 8.4 million below level 1, while 8.2 million could not participate in PIAAC's background survey either because of a language barrier or a cognitive or physical inability to be interviewed....By race/ethnicity and nativity status, the largest percentage of those with low literacy skills

Fig. 2.1 American flag

are White U.S.-born adults, who represent one-third of such a low-skilled population. Hispanic adults born outside the United States make up about a quarter of such low-skilled adults in the United States.

https://nces.ed.gov/datapoints/2019179.asp

As the article points out, something like 43 million Americans have low literacy skills, which suggests there is a deep divide between those who have attended colleges and universities and those who have not.

Many of those with low literacy skills are White US-born adults. Some immigrants to America may be quite literate in their native languages but not very literate in English. This low literacy rate has important implications for our politics and society.

A Note on American National Character

Americans are different from people in other countries and see themselves as different. But people in all countries see themselves as different from people in every other country. The Democratic and Republican Parties in the USA had an election and one of the important themes of both of the candidates was what we describe as "American exceptionalism," the notion that America is different from other countries and that by virtue of our unique spiritual values, economic wealth, and military power, we have a responsibility to "lead" the world in various ways.

On September 25, 2015, David Brooks, a columnist for *The New York Times*, had a column titled "The American Idea," which starts as follows:

> America was settled, founded, and built by people who believed they were doing something exceptional. Other nations were defined by their history, but America was defined by its future, by the people who weren't yet here and by the greatness that hadn't yet been achieved.

Later in the column, he argues that the conservative Republican politicians who talk about American exceptionalism are destroying the concept by looking backward to an imagined America, an America that was not multicultural and multiracial and that was not full of immigrants from Europe, Asia, and Africa and everyplace else.

The image of America in the minds of the Republican politicians Brooks was writing about is of a fantasied America made up primarily of WASPS (White Anglo-Saxon Protestants) living in farms and small towns and not in an America with huge cities full of people from many other countries with many different skin colors, languages, and religions. Nowadays, more than sixty percent of Americans live in cities and only seven percent of Americans live on farms.

Anyone who has traveled to countries in Europe, Asia, and South America can tell you people in the various countries in these continents are all different from one another in various ways such as their skin color and body shapes, the languages they speak, the food they eat, the clothes they wear, the way they have sex, their racial makeup, and the religions they practice.

The term we use for the differences we find in countries as far as personality is concerned is national character. What national character suggests is that where we are born and grow up plays an important role in the way we think and behave.

Nations differ from one another in various ways and parts or regions of countries differ from other parts of the same country in important ways. I recall reading a description of a book by a geographer who argued that there are seven different Americas, such as the New England America, Pacific Northwest America, Midwest America, Deep South America, Atlantic States of America (such as New York and New Jersey), and so on. So place matters and has an effect when it comes to national character.

CLOTAIRE RAPAILLE ON *THE CULTURE CODE* (FIG. 2.2)

A French psychoanalyst and marketing consultant, Clotaire Rapaille, wrote a book in 2006 that helps us understand how countries differ. His book is titled *The Culture Code: An Ingenious Way to Understand Why People Around the World Live and Buy as They Do*. In this book, he suggests that children from the age of one to seven are "imprinted" by the places in which they grow up and this imprinting helps shape their behavior for the rest of their lives.

He writes (2006, p. 21):

> Most of us imprint the meanings of the things most central to our lives by the age of seven. This is because emotion is the central force for children under the age of seven.

Rapaille believes that three kinds of unconscious shape our behavior: a Freudian individual unconscious, a Jungian collective unconscious, and a cultural unconscious, which represents the national codes imprinted on us that

Fig. 2.2 Clotaire Rapaille

shape our behavior. He explains the relationship that exists between codes as imprints (2006, p. 11):

> An imprint and its Code are like a lock and its combination. If you have all the right numbers in the right sequence, you can open the lock. Doing so over a vast array of imprints has profound implications. It brings to us the answer to one of our most fundamental questions: why do we act the way we do? Understanding the Culture Code provides us with a remarkable new tool—a new set of glasses, if you will, with which to view ourselves and our behaviors. It changes the way we see everything around us. What's more, it confirms what we have always suspected is true—that, despite our common humanity, people around the world really *are* different. *The Culture Code* offers a way to understand how.

The Culture Code discusses the differences between Americans and people in other cultures. They all have been imprinted by different national codes that affect their behavior. This explains why the children of immigrants become Americans so easily. If they are young enough, they become "imprinted" with American cultural codes. For their older brothers and sisters, the process is a bit more difficult, but human beings are very adaptable, and if they attend our schools, they usually can learn the codes and adapt.

Since their parents have been imprinted with the codes of the country where they grew up and lived, it is more difficult for them to adjust to American culture—but it is not impossible and millions of immigrants in America have integrated themselves into the fabric of American society. This is not the case in France where the Muslim immigrants, for a variety of reasons, have not been integrated very well into French culture.

One of the most interesting differences, Rapaille notes, is reflected in the way American and French people relate to cheese. The American code for cheese is "dead" and so they wrap it in plastic and store it in morgues known as refrigerators. The French code for cheese is "alive" so the French store their cheese in containers (cloches) and don't put cheese in the refrigerator.

What is important to realize is that every culture has its codes and finding the codes that inform each culture helps us understand why people in that culture act the way they do. Rapaille says that the American code for food is FUEL because we regard the body as a machine that must be kept going. That explains why at the end of a meal in America we say "I'm full," while in France, where people have a different attitude toward food, people say "that was delicious." He points out that in 2005 Americans spent a hundred billion dollars on fast food, though he does recognize that there are some "foodies" in the USA.

There are, then, different codes for different activities in each country and young children are "imprinted" with the codes and these codes generally guide their behavior for the rest of their lives. These codes can be described as "the way we do things here" and there are also codes in France, China, Japan, wherever, and what we call culture can be understood to be the numerous codes that are imprinted upon us as we grow up. It is possible, of course, for people to move to other countries and learn and adapt to different codes, but for the most part, the way we live as Americans, Germans, or Japanese is based on the codes we learned as we grew up in America, Germany, or Japan (Fig. 2.3).

Fig. 2.3 Geoffrey Gorer

Geoffrey Gorer on How Cultures Maintain Themselves

Geoffrey Gorer, an English anthropologist, discusses national character in his book *The People of Great Russia: A Psychological Study*. He writes, in the introduction to the book, about the way cultures maintain themselves (1962, pp. xxix–xxxx):

> If we accept the fact that all the peoples of the world are human, with the same physiology and the same psychological potentialities, whatever their present level of technological development, system of values, or political organization, and that all human beings are organized into societies with distinctive cultures, then all human beings and human societies can be studied, at least potentially, by scientific techniques which have been developed to these ends. Of these scientific techniques, social anthropology and whole-person psychology (including depth psychology and developmental data of ethology) are the most appropriate. Psychology has shown that in the life of any individual the process of learning is cumulative, so that early learning influences later learning; social anthropology has shown that culture is continuous over more than one generation, that the people who die are replaced by new members who have learned, by both conscious and unconscious processes, the values and customs appropriate to their culture and their position in it, or, in other words, their individual variation of the national character.

Rapaille and Gorer offer us valuable insights into how individuals become socialized and how cultures maintain themselves.

The Complexities of Everyday Life

Where one is born plays an important role in shaping our everyday lives, but there are many other factors, demographic and psychographic such as:

The Region in the Country And City Where One Is Raised
Americans may be generally alike as far as national character is concerned, but people raised in New York are different from people raised in the Deep South in terms of everything from their accents to what they eat. And people raised in Brooklyn are different from those raised in Manhattan. New Yorkers and Bostonians are very different in many ways. In short, variations are infinite and regional variations are important.

The following topics play an important role in helping us develop an identity and shaping our behavior:

Age
The everyday life of babies and toddlers is different from the everyday lives of preteens, teenagers, adolescents, 30-year-olds, middle-aged people, old people, and very old people. It is estimated that there are 573,000 Americans older than 100 years of age in 2021.

Gender
The old bi-polar way of looking at gender (either male or female) is now seen as obsolete and gender is regarded as a kind of performance open to many variations. We now find many people in America in various stages of transition from male to female or vice versa and with other gender identifications. Gender, then, is fluid.

Ethnicity
America is a nation of immigrants with people from many different countries, who have brought their beliefs, cuisines, cultural beliefs, religions, and other things with them. Thus we have Irish-Americans, Iranian-Americans, Italian-Americans, Jewish-Americans, and so on. According to the American Immigration Council, "Today, 14 percent of the nation's residents are foreign-born, over half of whom are naturalized U.S. citizens. Nearly 70 percent of all immigrants, who come from diverse backgrounds across the globe, report speaking English well or very well." Accessed 12/13/2021.

Race
It is widely accepted that antagonism to people of color informs many areas of American culture. For example, white nationalism is an important political force in contemporary America. Because there are so many mixed marriages in recent years, it is difficult at times to say that a person is an African American or any other kind of blended American.

Religion
Our religions play an important role in our development. America is generally described as a Christian nation, but there are large numbers of Jews and Muslims and people who follow other religions living in the country. And many people are not religious.

Socio-Economic Status
Our socio-economic status shapes the way we raise our children, our lifestyles, where we live, and the role we play in society. Kings have different lifestyles than peasants and billionaires have different lifestyles than members of the middle class. We realized that America is not a classless, all-middle-class country with just pockets of poverty. Income inequality is a major problem in America and has remained a problem for many years.

Occupation
There is generally a correlation between people's occupations and their status and lifestyles. Doctors, dentists, and people with advanced degrees have more status and prestige and, as a rule, higher incomes than people who have not graduated from high school or colleges and universities.

Cultural Capital
This term relates to the level of cultural sophistication people have and their "taste," and is connected to their education and socio-economic status. We identify this term with the thinking of the French sociologist of taste, Pierre Bourdieu.

Politics
People's politics are generally connected to their educational attainments, socio-economic status, religions and religious beliefs, and occupations. People tend to want to live in places where people with similar political beliefs live and associate with people with similar political beliefs. We do this to avoid cognitive dissonance and to find reinforcement in our social and political beliefs.

Personality Factors
Some people are introverts and others are extroverts and most people are neither but closer to one extreme or the other. Personality factors play an important role in our lives: in our occupations, in our choice of partners, and in our social relationships. The term "personal" means "mask," so it may be that our personalities are really social performances. Some thinkers make a distinction between personality and character.

And so on, ad infinitum.

Since this is a book about everyday life in postmodern America, I thought it would be useful to provide some information about American character, society, and culture. This enables readers to make useful inferences about everyday life in America.

The way I live in Mill Valley, a small town very close to San Francisco, is quite different from the way I would have lived if I have taken jobs offered to me, when I received my Ph.D., in Carbondale, Illinois (known, because of its hot summers, as "little Egypt") or, in Tampa, Florida.

There are around 7 billion people in the world and we are all alike in many respects, but we have evolved nations, cultures, and subcultures that are, in many respects, very different from one another. When you add the demographic and psychographic factors in our lives, you can see how complicated people are and why it is so difficult for social scientists to understand human behavior, at every level.

REFERENCES

Brooks, David. 2015, Sept 25. The American idea. *The New York Times.*
Gorer, Geoffrey, and John Rickman. 1962. *The people of great Russia: A psychological study.* New York: W. W. Norton.
Miner, Horace. 1956. Body ritual among the Nacirema. *American Anthropologist.* 58 (3): 503–507.
Rapaille, Clotaire. 2006. *The culture code: An ingenious way to understand why people around the world live and buy as they do.* New York, NY: Broadway Books.

CHAPTER 3

A Cultural Studies Analysis of Everyday Life

Chapter Objectives In this chapter, the four basic methodologies of cultural studies are introduced: semiotics theory, Marxist theory, psychoanalytic theory, and sociological theory. Each section on theory discusses some of its basic concepts and offers quotations from major thinkers in each methodology. Thus, in semiotics, the basic concerns of semiotics are examined; the work of Ferdinand de Saussure, Charles Sanders Peirce, and others is considered; and key statements in semiotic theory are offered.

We find the same organization in the discussion of Marxist theory, where the work of the French Marxist semiotician is discussed, in the section on psychoanalytic theory, where Freud's topographic theory and his structural hypothesis are explained, and in the section on sociological theory, where the ideas and writings of Emile Durkheim, Pierre Bourdieu, Georg Simmel, and Max Weber are dealt with.

Keywords Semiotic theory • Psychoanalytic theory • Marxist theory • Sociological theory

> Cultural studies is an innovative interdisciplinary field of research and teaching that investigates the ways in which "culture" creates and transforms individual experiences, everyday life, social relations and power. Research and teaching in the field explores the relations between culture understood as human expressive and symbolic activities, and cultures understood as distinctive ways of life. Combining the strengths of the social sciences and the humanities, cultural studies draws on methods and theories from literary
>
> *(continued)*

© The Author(s), under exclusive license to Springer Nature Switzerland AG 2022
A. A. Berger, *Everyday Life in the Postmodern World*, Springer Texts in Social Sciences, https://doi.org/10.1007/978-3-031-07926-9_3

> **continued**
> studies, sociology, communications studies, history, cultural anthropology, and economics. By working across the boundaries among these fields, cultural studies addresses new questions and problems of today's world. Rather than seeking answers that will hold for all time, cultural studies develops flexible tools that adapt to this rapidly changing world.

> Cultural life is not only concerned with symbolic communication, it is also the domain in which we set collective tasks for ourselves and begin to grapple with them as changing communities. Cultural studies is devoted to understanding the processes through which societies and the diverse groups within them come to terms with history, community life, and the challenges of the future.

> http://culturalstudies.web.unc.edu/resources-2/what-is-cultural-studies/

> **Cultural studies**, interdisciplinary field concerned with the role of social institutions in the shaping of culture. Cultural studies emerged in Britain in the late 1950s and subsequently spread internationally, notably to the United States and Australia. Originally identified with the Center for Contemporary Cultural Studies at the University of Birmingham (founded 1964) and with such scholars as Richard Hoggart, Stuart Hall, and Raymond Williams, cultural studies later became a well-established field in many academic institutions.

> https://www.britannica.com/topic/cultural-studies

My Ph.D. is in American Studies, an interdisciplinary approach to studying and analyzing various aspects of American culture and, here, in this book, American everyday life. In recent years, I've identified myself as a cultural studies scholar. It is, like American Studies, an interdisciplinary approach—but to all kinds of topics of interest to its practitioners. The four core disciplines in cultural studies, as I see things, are semiotics, psychoanalytic theory, Marxist theory, and sociological theory, though cultural studies scholars use other disciplines in their research such as anthropological theory and history. I offer primers on these four basic cultural studies sciences, starting with semiotics.

Semiotic Theory and Everyday Life

Let me begin with the following quotation by Mark Gottdiener, which explains the basics of semiotics. It is found in his book *The Theming of America: Dreams, Visions, and Commercial Spaces* (1997, pp. 8, 9):

> The basic unit of semiotics is the *sign* defined conceptually as something that stands for something else, and, more technically, as a spoken or written word, a drawn figure, or a material object unified in the mind with a particular cultural concept. The sign is this unity of word-object, known as a *signifier* with a corresponding, culturally prescribed content or meaning, known as a *signified*. Thus our minds attach the word "dog," or the drawn figure of a "dog," as a signifier to the idea of a "dog," that is, a domesticated canine species possessing certain behavioral characteristics. If we came from a culture that did not possess dogs in daily life, however unlikely, we would not know what the signifier "dog" means.... When dealing with objects that are signifiers of certain concepts, cultural meanings, or ideologies of belief, we can consider them not only as "signs," but *sign vehicles*. Signifying objects carry meanings with them.

Daniel Chandler discusses the relationship that exists between signs and codes in his book *Semiotics: The Basics* (2002, p. 147):

> Since the meaning of a sign depends on the code within which it is situated, codes provide a framework within which signs make sense. Indeed, we cannot grant something the status of a sign if it does not function within a code....The conventions of codes represent a social dimension in semiotics: a code is a set of practices familiar to users of the medium operating with a broad cultural framework.... When studying cultural practices, semioticians treat as signs any objects or actions which have meaning to the members of a cultural group, seeking to identify the rules or conventions of the codes which underlie the production of meaning within that culture.

Even though you may never have heard the term "semiotics," I would suggest that you've been a semiotician all your life. That's because you've spent every moment you've been awake (and if Freud is correct when dreaming) involved with making sense of the world. Semiotics, technically speaking the science of signs, deals with how we find meaning in our everyday activities and all our experiences.

One of the founding fathers of semiotics, a Harvard professor named Charles Sanders Peirce, said that the universe is full of signs if not made entirely of them. If everything is a sign, semiotics becomes the master science that enables us to interpret these signs—a sign being anything that can be used to stand for something else. Words are signs, so when you learned what words mean, as a little child, and later, when you learned to read, you started your career as a semiotician.

Our facial expressions are signs. For example, a smile is a sign of some kind of feeling. Generally, we interpret a smile to mean a mood like pleasure or friendliness, but it can also mean just the opposite. We have to learn how to interpret signs and we do this as we grow up and better understand what signs like smiles have to tell us.

Poker players look for signs—they call them "tells"—which provide information about the hand a player has. That is why poker players learn to develop a "poker face" which provides no information to other players. In some cases, a sign can be very minute, as, for example, when the pupils of a poker player's eyes dilate (get enlarger), an involuntary response that signifies that something has excited the player: a good card or a bad card. Poker players are master applied semioticians. In addition to facial expressions, they look for signs such as body language, facial coloring, perspiration, nervousness, and so on.

Reading People

When we "read" people, either in real life or when watching them on videos or films, here are some of the things we look at, often in just a momentary glance:

Height	Size and shape of ears
Body shape: thin, medium, fat, obese	Neck size and length
Skin color	Facial expressions
Race	Neck length
Ethnicity	Hat style (if wearing a hat)
Complexion	Gestures
Gender	Hands (rings?)
Hairstyle	Fingernails
Hair color	Handbags, briefcases, backpacks, etc.
Color of eyes	Style of clothes
Eyeglasses style and brand (when evident)	Brands of clothes (when evident)
Ear jewelry	Color of clothes
Nose jewelry	Fabric of clothes
Lips (thin, fleshy)	Neckwear (if any)
Teeth straightness and color	Kind of tie and knot used for men's ties
Chin structure: receding? prognathous (jutting chin)?	Jackets, coats, outerwear
Size of nose	Kind of shoes
Shape of the nose (straight, hooked)?	Style of shoes

My point is that we are all like poker players, observing people, and trying to determine what their facial expressions, gestures, body language, and all their other signs tell us about them.

Ferdinand de Saussure (Fig. 3.1)

Semiotics is the science that studies how we find meaning in signs. There are two founding fathers of semiotics. One is the Swiss linguist Ferdinand de Saussure (1857–1913) whose lectures were turned into a highly influential book by two of his students, *Course in General Linguistics*. It was published in French in 1915 and translated into English in 1966. As Saussure explained (1966, pp. 66–67):

> The linguistic sign unites not a thing and a name but a concept and a sign-image....I call the combination of a concept and a sign image a *sign*, but in current usage the term generally designates only a sound-image.

Fig. 3.1 Ferdinand de Saussure

Saussure divided signs into two parts: a sign-image, which he called a *signifier*, and a concept, which he called a *signified*. The relationship that exists between signifiers and signified is arbitrary, a matter of convention.

Saussure offered what we might describe as one of the charter statements of the study of signs (1966, p. 16):

> Language is a system of signs that express ideas, and is therefore comparable to a system of writing, the alphabet of deaf-mutes, symbolic rites, polite formulas, military signals, etc. But it is the most important of all these systems.
> *A science that studies the life of signs within society* is conceivable; it would be a part of social psychology and consequently of general psychology; I shall call it *semiology* (from Greek *sēmeîon* "sign"). Semiology would show what constitutes signs, what laws govern them. Since the science does not yet exist, no one can say what it would be; but it has a right to existence, a place staked out in advance.

The italics were in the original. What Saussure suggests is that semiology would study signs and figure out how to analyze them. He also offered an important insight relative to our understanding of concepts. He explained that concepts have meaning because of relationships, and the basic relationship is oppositional Thus, "healthy" doesn't mean anything unless there is "sick," or "happy" unless there is "sad." He added (1966, p.117)

> Concepts are purely differential and defined not by their positive content but negatively by their relations with the other terms of the system.

It is not the "content" of a concept that determines its meaning, but "relations" among concepts in some kind of a system.

This leads to his conclusion that (1966, p. 117) "[the] most precise characteristic" of these concepts "is in being what the others are not." "Signs function," he adds (1966, p. 118), "not through their intrinsic value but through their relative position." In essence, we determine the meaning of a concept by recognizing what it is not.

We can see this readily enough in language, but it also holds for texts of all kinds. Nothing has meaning in itself!

Charles Sanders Peirce (Fig. 3.2)

Saussure called his science semiology, basing it on the Greek term for a sign, *sēmeîon*. The other founding father of semiotics, the American philosopher Charles Sanders Peirce (1839–1914), called his science of signs semiotics and that has become the term used by almost everyone involved with the study and analysis of signs. Peirce wrote that there are three kinds of signs: icons, indexes, and symbols. *Icons* signify by resemblance, *indexes* signify by cause and effect, and *symbols* signify based on convention. As Peirce wrote (Quoted in J. J. Zeman, "Pierce's Theory of Signs," in T. S. Sebeok (Ed.) *A Perfusion of Signs.* Bloomington: Indiana University Press.) (1977, p. 36).

> Every sign is determined by its objects, either first by partaking in the characters of the object, when I call a sign an *Icon;* secondly, by being really and in its individual existence connected with the individual object, when I call the sign an *Index;* thirdly, by more or less approximate certainty that it will be interpreted as denoting the object, in consequence of a habit (which term I use as including a natural disposition), when I call the sign a *Symbol.*

We can see their relationships in the chart that follows (Table 3.1):

Fig. 3.2 Charles Sanders Peirce

Table 3.1 Peirce's analysis of kinds of signs

	Icons	*Indexes*	*Symbols*
Signify by	Resemblance	Cause and effect	Convention
Example	Photograph	Fire and smoke	Cross, flag
Process	See	Figure out	Learn

There are, of course, many other aspects to semiotic thought, but with these two understandings of the sign, and a few others we can start making applied semiotic analyses.

What Saussure and Peirce do is enable us to understand how people find meaning in things in their everyday lives. Peirce also put the interpreter of signs in the middle of things. As he wrote (also quoted in Zeman, 1977, p. 27), a sign is "something which stands to somebody for something in some respect or capacity." If we combine Saussure's notions about signs and Peirce's writings on signs we have a repertoire of tools that will help us understand how signs generate meaning.

Amazon.com's bookstore has more than 22,000 books on semiotics and Google has 10,400,000 results (accessed 12/1/2021) if you type "semiotics" in Google Search. There is a lot of interest in semiotics because it is so useful to people—not only poker players but also people who find themselves surrounded by signs and want to understand what the signs mean and reveal in our everyday lives.

Signs have a lot to tell us if we know how to ask them the right questions. Maya Pines, a journalist, describes this process as follows ("How They Know What You Really Mean," *San Francisco Chronicle,* Oct 13, 1982):

> Everything we do sends messages about us in a variety of codes, semiologists contend. We are also on the receiving end of innumerable messages encoded in music, gestures, foods, rituals, books, movies, or advertisements. Yet we seldom realize that we have received such messages, and would have trouble explaining the rules under which they operate.

Thus, semiotics helps us understand how to decipher the messages we are sent by others and understand better the messages we send about ourselves to others. We're often unaware of the messages we're sending and how others are interpreting them and we often make mistakes in interpreting the signs that others are sending us.

Semiotics is important since "everything we do," as Pines put it, involves sending messages about ourselves to others and interpreting messages others send us.

Key Statements by Semiotic Theorists

I offer now some important or "key" statements by semiotics theorists that will further our understanding of semiotics.

This Universe Is Perfused with Signs

> It seems a strange thing, when one comes to ponder over it, that a sign should leave its interpreter to supply part of its meaning; but the explanation of the phenomenon lies in the fact that the entire universe—not merely the universe of existents, but all that wider universe, embracing the universe of existents, as a part, the universe which we are all accustomed to refer to as "the truth"—that all this universe is perfused with signs if it not composed exclusively of signs.
>
> C.S. Peirce. Epigraph in T. Sebeok. *A Perfusion of Signs*. Bloomington: Indiana University Press. 1977.

Signs and Lies (Fig. 3.3)

> Semiotics is concerned with everything that can be taken as a sign. A sign is everything which can be taken as significantly substituting for something else. This something else does not necessarily have to exist or to actually be somewhere at the moment in which a sign stands for it. Thus semiotics is in principle the discipline studying everything which can be used in order to lie. If something cannot be used to tell a lie, conversely it cannot be used to tell the truth; it cannot be used "to tell" at all.

Fig. 3.3 Umberto Eco

Umberto Eco. *A Theory of Semiotics.* Bloomington: Indiana University Press. 1976.

All Cultural Objects Convey Meaning

The underlying argument behind the semiotic approach is that, since all cultural objects convey meaning, and all cultural practices depend on meaning, they must make use of signs; and in so far as they do, they must work like language works, and be amenable to an analysis which basically makes us of Saussure's linguistic concepts...his idea of underlying codes and structures, and the arbitrary nature of the sign. Thus, when in his collection of essays, *Mythologies* (1972), the French critic Roland Barthes, studies "The world of wrestling," "soap powders and detergents," "The Face of Greta Garbo," or The *Blue Guides* to Europe," he brought a semiotic approach to bear on "reading" popular culture, treating these activities and objects as signs, as a language through which meaning is communicated.

Stuart Hall, ed. *Representation: Cultural Representations and Signifying Practices.* London: Sage Publications. 1997.

Semiotics and Tourism

I have suggested that tourist attractions are signs....Sightseers do not, in any empirical sense, see San Francisco. They see Fisherman's Wharf, a cable car, the Golden Gate Bridge, Union Square, Coit Tower, the Presidio, City Lights Bookstore, Chinatown, and perhaps the Haight Ashbury or a nude go-go dancer in a North Beach-Barbary Coast club.

Dean MacCannell, *The Tourist: A New Theory of the Leisure Class.* New York: Schocken Books. 1976.

Signs and Everyday Life

If you allow the swarms of signs to flow over you from television and radio sets, from films and newspaper and ratify the commentaries that determine their meanings, you will become the passive victim of the situation; but insert a distinction or two—for instance everyday life and modernity—and the situation is changed: you are now an active interpreter of signs.

Henri Lefebvre. *Everyday Life in the Modern World.*
Trans. Sacha Rabinovich. New York: Harper & Row. 1971.

This material covers many important aspects of semiotics and provides you with concepts that can help you make a semiotic analysis of everyday life. We turn now to Marxist theory (Fig. 3.4).

Fig. 3.4   Karl Marx

The Marxist Analysis of Everyday Life

One of the best descriptions of what Marxism has to say about everyday life appears in an article by Donald Lazere, "Mass culture, political consciousness, and English Studies" in *College English* (1977, 38, pp. 755–756):

> Applied to any aspect of culture, Marxist method seems to explicate the manifest and latent or coded reflections of modes of material production, ideological value, class relations and structures of social power racial or sexual as well as politico economic or the state of consciousness of people in a precise historical or socio-economic situation. . . . The Marxist method, recently in varying degrees of combination with structuralism and semiology, has provided an incisive analytic tool for studying the political signification in every facet of contemporary culture, including popular entertainment in TV and films, music, mass circulation books, newspaper and magazine features, comics, fashion, tourism, sports and games, as well as such acculturating institutions as education, religion, the family and child rearing, social and sexual relations between men and women, all the patterns of work, play, and other customs of everyday life. . . . The most frequent theme in Marxist cultural criticism is the way the prevalent mode of production and ideology of the ruling class in any society dominate every phase of culture, and at present, the way capitalist production and ideology dominate American culture, along with that of the rest of the world that American business and culture have colonized.

What we learn from Lazere is that Marxists have interesting and important things to say about the role of ideology in just about every aspect of "contemporary culture" or, in our terms, everyday life (Fig. 3.5).

One of the most influential Marxist thinkers (and semiotician) in the twentieth century was the French scholar, Roland Barthes, author of a classic study of applied Marxist semiotics, *Mythologies,* and other works on semiotics, advertising, literary theory, and various aspects of everyday life. In his preface to the 1972 edition of *Mythologies,* Barthes writes (1972, p. 9):

Fig. 3.5 Roland Barthes

I had just read Saussure and as a result acquired the conviction that by treating "collective representations" as sign systems, one might hope to go further than the pious show of unmasking them and account *in detail* for the mystification which transforms petit-bourgeois culture into a universal nature.

We can regard Barthes' *Mythologies* as not only a Marxist semiotic analysis of French culture but also as an example of an analysis of marketing and everyday life in France. Thus, for example, he discusses the meaning of soap powders and detergents to people in France—whose ideological significance is something of which they may not be aware (1972, pp. 36–37):

Chlorinated fluids, for instance, have always been experienced as a sort of liquid fire, the action of which must be carefully estimated, otherwise the object itself would be affected, "burnt"…This type of product rests on the idea of a violent, abrasive modification of matter…the product "kills" the dirt. Powders, on the contrary, are separating agents: their ideal role is to liberate the object from its circumstantial imperfection: dirt is "forced out" and no longer killed. in the *Omo* imagery, dirt is a diminutive enemy, stunted and black, which takes to its heels from the fine immaculate linen at the sole threat of a judgment of *Omo*….To say that *Omo* cleans in depth…is to assume that linen is deep, which no one had previously thought, and this unquestionably results in exalting it….

If you know what soaps and detergents "mean" to people, you can develop an advertising campaign that will be more effective than one which does not recognize their meanings—even if the members of the target audience are not aware of these meanings at the conscious level.

This passage also suggests the utility of using other modes of analysis—in this case, psychoanalytic theory—along with Marxism and semiotics in analyzing texts and other aspects of everyday life. In *Mythologies,* Barthes has chapters on many aspects of everyday life in France such as "Wine and Milk," "Steak and Chips," "Operation Margarine," "Toys," and "Plastic."

Marxist theories offer a powerful tool for analyzing how the "ruling classes," who control the economic institutions of society, shape the consciousness of the masses, what Marx called "the proletariat." Marx focused upon the class makeup of societies and of the way those at the top of the socio-economic pyramid maintained their position of dominance. We find Marxist theories informing the work of the French critic Henri Lefebvre, the English critic John Berger, the German critic Walter Benjamin, and numerous other culture analysts. Although most modern-day Marxists may not believe in violent revolution, they still use his concepts to offer their critiques of the deficiencies of contemporary bourgeois capitalist societies.

Key Statements by Marxist Theorists

Here are some quotations from Marx and Marxists that show some of the basic ideas of Marxist theory:

The Ruling Classes

> The ideas of the ruling class are, in every age, the ruling ideas: i.e. the class which is the dominant material force in society is at the same time the dominant intellectual force. The class which has the means of material production at its disposal, has control at the same time over the means of mental production.
> Karl Marx, *Selected Writings in sociology and social philosophy.* (T.B. Bottomore & M. Rubel, Eds. T.B. Bottomore, transl. New York: McGraw-Hill. 1964

Class Conflict

> The history of all hitherto existing societies is the history of class struggles. Freeman and slave, patrician and plebeian, lord and serf, guild-master and journeyman, in a word oppressor and oppressed, stood in constant opposition to one another, carried on an uninterrupted, now hidden, now open, fight, a fight that each time ended either in a revolutionary reconstitution of society at large, or in the common ruin of the contending classes.
> Karl Marx, *Selected Writings in Sociology and Social Philosophy.* (Transl. T.B. Bottomore). New York: McGraw-Hill. 1964.

The Base and the Superstructure (Fig. 3.6)

> The economic structure of society always furnishes the real basis, starting from which we can alone work out the ultimate explanation of the whole superstruc-

Fig. 3.6 Theodor W. Adorno

ture of juridical and political institutions as well as of the religious, philosophical, and other ideas of a given historical period.

Friedrich Engels, *Socialism: Utopian and Scientific,* in R. Tucker, Ed. *The Marx-Engels Reader.* New York: W.W. Norton. 1972

Mass Culture

Rigid institutionalism transforms modern mass culture into a medium of undreamed psychological control. The repetitiveness, the selfsameness, and the ubiquity of modern mass culture tend to make for automatized reactions and to weaken the forces of individual resistance.

Theodor W. Adorno, *Philosophy of Modern Music.* New York: Seabury. 1948.

The Role of the Proletariat

The overthrow of bourgeois rule can be accomplished only by the proletariat, as the particular class, which, by the economic conditions of its existence, is being prepared for this work and is provided with the opportunity and the power to perform it...The doctrine of the class struggle, as applied by Marx to the question of the state and of the Socialist revolution, leads inevitably to the recognition of the *political rule* of the proletariat, of its dictatorship, i.e., of a power shared with none and relying directly upon the armed force of the masses. The overthrow of the bourgeoisie is realisable only by the transformation of the proletariat into the *ruling class,* able to crush the inevitable and desperate resistance of the bourgeoisie, and to organize, for the new economic order, *all* the toiling and exploited masses.

Vladimir Lenin. *State and Revolution.* 1932. New York: International Publishers.

Alienation

The alienation of the worker from his product means not only that his labour becomes an object, takes on its own existence, but that it exists outside him, independently, and alien to him, and that it stands opposed to him as an autonomous power. The life which he has given to the object sets itself against him as an alien and hostile force.

Karl Marx, *Karl Marx, Selected Writings in sociology and social philosophy.* (T.B. Bottomore & M. Rubel, Eds. T.B. Bottomore, transl.) New York: McGraw-Hill. 1964.

Ideology

The ideological processes that determine political candidates as well as products are hidden, argue critical scholars. Media influence, for Hall and neo-Marxist scholars in general, is not in overt "messages" but in the ideological structuring or values and beliefs that shape or constrain the message. Ideology is evidenced in the taken for granted, the assumed, the "common sense" of a situation; it is what is not said, because it "goes without saying." It works by excluding what cannot be imagined or thought because it seems too bizarre or absurd or beyond the pale.

Joli Jensen. *Redeeming Modernity: Contradictions in Media Criticism.* London: Sage. 1990.

Byt

Originally, *byt* simply referred to everyday existence or a way of life shared in a community. It was opposed to *bytie,* the spiritual sphere....Under the influence of the symbolists, the intelligentsia, including early revolutionaries, infused it with connotations of banality, "stagnation and routine, of daily transience without transcendence, whether spiritual, artistic or revolutionary." *Byt,* the ordinary way of life, began to be seen as the order of chaos and contingency that precludes any illumination.

Annie Gerin, *Devastation and Laughter: Satire, Power, and Culture in the Early Soviet State, 1920s–1930s.* Toronto: University of Toronto Press.

Postmodernism

Postmodernism is not the cultural dominant of a wholly new social order (the rumor about which, under the name of "postindustrial society," ran through the media a few years ago, but only the reflex and the concomitant of yet another systematic modification of capitalism itself.

Fredric Jameson, *Postmodernism or, The Cultural Logic of Late Capitalism*

Fig. 3.7 *Bloom's Morning*

These quotations furnish us with some of the basic ideas of Marxism and Marxist thinkers that we can apply to our analysis of everyday life in America and elsewhere as well (Fig. 3.7).

For those interested in an extended cultural studies, semiotic, and Marxist analysis of everyday life in America, I have written a book, *Bloom's Morning: Coffee, Comforters, and the Secret Meaning of Everyday Life* that has 36 chapters on everything from clock radios and toasters to get toothpaste and trash compactors. It also discusses why everyday life is an important topic for analysis by cultural studies scholars (Fig. 3.8).

Psychoanalytic Theory and Everyday Life

When Barthes writes, in *Mythologies,* about linen being "deep," he is alluding to the fact that many things that are part of our everyday lives have meanings of which we are unaware, which suggests the importance of our next theory, classical Freudian psychoanalytic thought.

Freud's Topographic Hypothesis

One of Freud's most important ideas involves his theory about the unconscious. This is known as his "topographic hypothesis." Freud wrote (quoted in P. Rieff, ed. *Character and Culture* 1910/1963, pp. 235–236):

> It was a triumph of the interpretative art of psychoanalysis when it succeeded in demonstrating that certain common mental acts of normal people, for which no

Fig. 3.8 Sigmund Freud

one had hitherto attempted to put forward a psychological explanation, were to be regarded in the same light as the symptoms of neurotic: that is to say they had a *meaning*, which was unknown to the subject, but which could easily be discovered by analytic means…A class of material was brought to light which is calculated better than any other to stimulate a belief in the existence of unconscious mental acts even in people to whom the hypothesis of something at once mental and unconscious might seem strange and even absurd.

Freud explained that our psyches have three levels of consciousness:

Consciousness
What we are aware of in our minds

The Subconscious (also known as The Preconscious)
What we are dimly aware of.

The Unconscious
What is in our minds but the contents of which we are unaware and cannot access without help by psychologists and other kinds of professionals. I suggest that the psyche is like an iceberg and made a drawing of an iceberg that shows the relationships (Fig. 3.9).

Fig. 3.9 Iceberg simile for the psyche

The part of the iceberg we can see is our consciousness. The subconscious or preconscious is that area of the iceberg a few feet below the water that we can dimly make out. But most of the iceberg, shown in black, is our unconscious. What is important to recognize is that many of our decisions are affected by the contents of our unconscious and we are not as rational as we like to think they are.

Freud's Structural Hypothesis

There is another Freudian theory that needs to be discussed, namely his "structural hypothesis" which suggests that there are three powerful forces in the psyche, what he called the id, the ego, and the superego, which are constantly interacting with one another.

The id is a chaos of excitement and involves our impulses and desires. The superego can be equated with conscience and guilt, the approval or disapproval of our actions, and related concerns.

The ego involves reason, rationality, and good sense and mediates between the id and the superego. We need a certain amount of id if we are to be active and have energy and we need a certain amount of superego to make sure we aren't dominated by our ids and can behave responsibly. If either id or superego is too dominant, we usually find psychological problems and neurosis (Fig. 3.10).

We can use the id/ego/superego to make sense of many aspects of our daily lives—even though we may not recognize that something has an id, ego, or superego aspect to it (Table 3.2).

Freud wrote many books, on psychoanalysis, dreams, humor, group psychology, and so on and had many controversial theories, such as his writings on the Oedipus Complex. Although many psychologists argue that we are living in post-Freudian times, his ideas are still influential and psychoanalytic theory is one of the cornerstones of cultural studies.

Fig. 3.10 Id, ego, superego in the mind

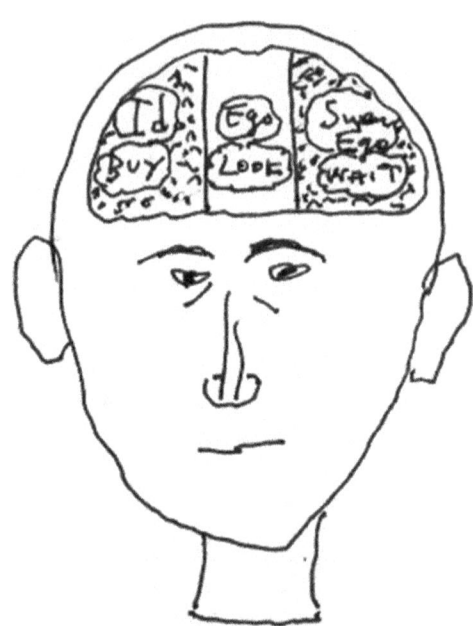

Table 3.2 Id, ego, and superego applied to society

Topic	ID	Ego	Superego
Book genres	Romances, Vampire novels	Textbooks	Bible, Koran
TV shows	Dancing with the Stars	Nature, Nova	Religious shows
Star Trek	McCoy	Spock	Kirk
Beverages	Champagne	Milk	Holy Water
Clothes	Bikini	Suit	Clerical garb

Key Statements by Psychoanalytic Theorists

Below I offer some quotations from important psychoanalytic theorists or writers who use psychoanalytic theory that will flesh out your understanding of the science.

Basic Elements of Psychoanalysis

Psychoanalysis is the name (1) of a procedure for the investigation of mental processes which are almost inaccessible any other way, (2) of a method (based upon that investigation) for the treatment of neurotic disorders and (3) of a collection of psychological information obtained along those lines which is gradually being accumulated into a new scientific discipline.

Sigmund Freud, *Character, and Culture*. Philip Rieff, Ed. New York: Collier Books. 1963.

The ID, the Ego, and the Superego

We may say that the id comprises the psychic representatives of the drives, the ego consists of those functions which have to do with the individual's relation to his environment, and the superego comprises the moral precepts of our minds as well as our ideal aspirations.
    Charles Brenner. *An Elementary Textbook of Psychoanalysis.* Garden City, NY: Doubleday. 1974.

The Symbolism of the Female Genitalia

The female genitalia are symbolically represented by all such objects as share with them the property of enclosing a space or are capable as acting as receptacles: such as pits, hollows and caves, and also jars and bottles, and boxes of all sorts and sizes, chests, coffers, pockets, and so forth. Ships too come into this category. Many symbols refer rather to the uterus than to all the other genital organs: thus cupboards, stoves and above all, rooms. Room symbolism here links up with that of houses, whilst doors and gates represent the genital opening…yet another noteworthy symbol of the female genital organ is a jewel case….
    Sigmund Freud, *A General Introduction to Psycho-Analysis.* New York: Washington Square Press. 1924.

Post-Freudian Psychoanalytic Theory

Very little of the way Freud understood and practiced psychoanalysis has remained simply intact. The major pillars of his theorizing--instinctual drives, the centrality of the Oedipus complex, the motivational primacy of sex and aggression--have all been challenged and fundamentally transformed in contemporary psychoanalytic thought. And Freud's basic technical principles--analytic neutrality, the systematic frustration of the patient's wishes, a regression of an infantile neurosis--have likewise been reconceptualized, revised, and transformed by current clinicians.
    Stephen A. Mitchell and Margaret J. Black. *Freud and Beyond: A History of Modern Psychoanalytic Thought.* New York: Basic Books. 1996.

Jung on Instincts

We do not assume that each newborn animal creates its own instincts as an individual acquisition, and we must not suppose that human individuals invent their specific human ways with every new birth. Like the instincts, the collective thought patterns of the human mind are innate and inherited. They function, when the occasion arises, in more or less the same way in all of us.
    Carl Jung. *Man and His Symbols.* Garden City, NY: Doubleday. 1964.

The Smallest Components of Everyday Life

Blink is concerned with the very smallest components of our everyday lives--the content and origin of those instantaneous impressions and conclusions that spontaneously arise whenever we meet a new person or confront a complex situation or have to make a decision under conditions of stress. When it comes to the task of understanding ourselves and our world, I think we pay too much attention to those grand themes and too little to the particulars of those fleeting moments. But what would happen if we took our instincts seriously? What if we stopped scanning the horizon with our binoculars and began instead examining our own decision making and behavior through the most powerful of microscopes?

Malcolm Gladwell, *blink. The Power of Thinking Without Thinking*. New York: Bay Back Books. 2005.

Freud's Influence

For the first five decades in the history of psychoanalytic thought (up until Freud's death in 1939), it would have been tenable to argue that psychoanalysis *was* largely the invention of Freud's singular genius. Freud regarded psychoanalysis as a form of treatment, but also as a new branch of science. He carefully ended his creation and it grew up around him. Those taught and analyzed by Freud were justifiably impressed with his early discoveries; they admired him and let him take the lead. Freud also regarded psychoanalysis as a quasi-political movement, and proved himself a dominant leader, wary of opposition, often regarding others' creativity and originality as signs of disloyalty.

Stephen A. Mitchell and Margaret J. Black. *Freud and Beyond: A History of Modern Psychoanalytic Thought*. New York: Basic Books. 1996.

Sociological Theory

There is some overlap between Marxist theory and sociological theory and we find that just as there are semiotic Marxists and psychoanalytic Marxists, there are Marxist sociologists and Marxist psychoanalysts.

Sociologists see human beings as social animals and focus their attention on the role of groups and institutions and in the process of socialization on human behavior. There are also political sociologists and many other mixtures in the social sciences (Fig. 3.11).

A French theorist, Auguste Comte (1798 to 1837), coined the term sociology and wrote that the goal of sociology is "to know in order to predict in order to control." He wanted to discover the laws that shaped people's lives so a more rational and humane society could be created (Fig 3.12).

Another French scholar Emile Durkheim (1858–1917) discussed the complex relationship that exists between individuals and society. As he explained in his book *The Elementary Forms of the Religious Life* (1915, p. 29):

> According to the well-known formula, man is double. There are two beings in him: an individual being which has its foundation in the organism and the circle of whose activities is therefore strictly limited, and a social being, which represents the highest reality in the intellectual and moral order that we can know by observation--I mean society. This duality of our nature has as its consequence in the practical order, the irreducibility of reason to individual experience. In so far

as he belongs to society, the individual transcends himself, both when he thinks and when he acts.

So we are members of society and, as a result, are "in" society, but society is "in" us since much of what we think and do is affected by our being a member of society. Our ideas about who we are and what life is like, and how we should behave, are shaped by this duality (Fig. 3.13).

Fig. 3.11 Auguste Comte

Fig. 3.12 Emile Durkheim

Fig. 3.13 Pierre Bourdieu

A more contemporary French sociologist, Pierre Bourdieu (1930–2002), who was a professor at the College de France, takes Durkheim's idea ad pushes it further, arguing that what we consider to be very personal, our taste, is socially constructed. He writes in his book *Sociology in Question* (1993, p. 27):

> Sociology reveals that the idea of personal opinion (like the idea of personal taste) is an illusion. From this, it is concluded that sociology is reductive, that it disenchants, that it demobilizes people by taking away all their illusions…If it is true that the idea of personal opinion itself is socially determined, that it is a product of history reproduced by education, that our opinions are determined, then it is better to know this; and if we have some chance of having personal opinions, it is perhaps on condition that we know our opinions are not spontaneously so.

It is very difficult for people to recognize that their opinions and taste are, to a considerable degree, shaped by society but that idea is central to many sociological theorists (Fig. 3.14).

Sociologists such as W. Lloyd Warner (1898–1970) have suggested that there are six basic social classes in the USA:

Upper-upper	1.4%
Lower-upper	1.6%
Upper-middle	10%
Lower-middle	28%
Upper-lower	33%
Lower-lower	25%

Fig. 3.14 W. Lloyd Warner

He suggests that the lower-middle and upper-lower classes formed what he called the common man (and woman) level. He did his work many years ago but his suggestion about the six basic classes is still valid, though the percentages of Americans in each class may have changed somewhat.

In recent years, the matter of income inequality of the classes, with the top one percent of the American public gaining immense wealth and the lower classes losing wealth, has become a serious problem.

In 2013, the British Broadcasting System surveyed classes in Britain and came up with seven social classes based on what they described as:

Economic capital   income, the value of a home and savings
Social capital   number of high-status people known
Cultural capital   elite cultural interests and activities

These terms were made popular by Pierre Bourdieu whose writings on distinction have been very influential.

The seven groups the survey found were:

Elites 6%
The most privileged class in Britain

Established middle class 25%
High levels of all capitals

Technical middle class 6%
High economic but low social and cultural capital

New affluent workers 15%
Medium level of economic but higher levels of social and cultural capital

Emergent service workers 19%
Low economic but higher levels of social and cultural capital

Traditional working class 14%
Low on all forms of capital

Precariat. Most deprived class 15%
Low levels of all capitals.

Britain and the USA are different in many ways, but this typology may have some usefulness in helping us understand class differences in America as well as in Britain (Fig. 3.15).

A German sociologist, Max Weber (1864 to 1920), made many contributions to sociological theory. He suggested that as societies became more complex, they needed to develop ways of controlling things and developed bureaucracies, which involved people following fixed rules and procedures for running institutions. Bureaucracies are characterized by having a hierarchical authority structure, impersonal ways of dealing with problems, and red tape. He argued that as societies became more complex, they changed from being led by charismatic leaders to bureaucrats running a rational-legal system.

As we look at many contemporary countries, led by autocrats and charismatic leaders, there is reason to suggest that Weber was too optimistic about the role of reason in politics. Weber was influenced, to some degree, by Marxist thinking. As Lewis A. Coser explains, in his book *Masters of Sociological Thought: Ideas in Historical ad Social Context* (1971, p. 250):

Fig. 3.15 Max Weber

Much of Weber's work, not only his sociology of ideas can best be understood as a continued interchange of ideas with Karl Marx. His theories of stratification and of economic behavior, for example, have their roots in Marxian economics and sociology. More generally, Weber admired Marx's hard-headed and matter-of-fact scholarship, his contempt for the cloudy "idealistic" mystifications of the German philosophical condition....Even when he criticized what he came to regard as Marx's overly simplified economic interpretation of history, he always remained respectful of Marx's intellectual eminence.

It isn't surprising that Weber was influenced by Marxist thought since Marx's writings have played an important role in the thinking of many sociologists and scholars in other disciplines to this day.

There are countless other topics that sociologists dealt with but there is one more that is important for us to consider—the topic of functionalism. Coser offers a discussion of functional explanation and provides a quotation from Emile Durkheim, the father of French sociology, who distinguishes between individual motivations and functional consequences (1971, p. 141):

When...the explanation of a social phenomenon is undertaken, we must seek separately the efficient cause which produces it and the function it fulfills. We use the word "function" in preference to "end" or "purpose," precisely because social phenomena do not generally exist for the useful results they produce. We must determine whether there is a correspondence between the fact under consideration and the general needs of the social organism, and in what the correspondence consists, without occupying ourselves with whether it was intentional or not.

[Note: This material on functionalism is from Durkheim's book *The Rules of Sociological Method*.]

Something is functional if it contributes to the stability and maintenance of some organization or entity or society. It is *dysfunctional* if it leads to the destruction or destabilization of the organization or entity or society. And it is *non-functional* if it plays no role in the maintenance of the entity organization or society.

Sociologists also distinguish between *manifest functions* that are based on conscious decisions and are recognized and *latent functions* that are not recognized and in many cases are the most important. Sociologists are also interested in what they describe as *functional alternatives*, which develop when an original institution is no longer effective and a substitute develops. Sociologists argue that institutions arise because certain things need to be done to maintain society. If the original institutions no longer are working well, a functional alternative becomes necessary to take its place.

Key Statements by Sociological Theorists

Below I offer some quotations from important sociological writers and theorists that provide insights into the science.

Society Is Primary

> For human beings, society is a primary reality, not just the sum of individual activities, not the contingent manifestations of Mind; and if one wishes to study human behavior, one must grant that there is a social reality. People live not simply among objects and actions but among objects and actions that have meaning, and these meanings cannot be treated as a sum of subjecting perceptions.... In short, sociology, linguistics, and psychoanalytic psychology are possible only when one takes meanings which are attached to and which differentiate objects and actions in society as a primary reality, as facts to be explained. And since meanings are a social product, explanations must be carried out in social terms.
>
> Jonathan Culler, *Ferdinand de Saussure*. (Revised edition). Ithaca, New York: Cornell University Press. 1986.

The Problem of Restraint

> It is not true...that human activity can be released from all restraint. Nothing in the world can enjoy such a privilege. All existence being a part of the universe is relative to the remainder; its nature and method of manifestation accordingly depend not only on itself but on other beings, who consequently restrain and regulate it. Here there are only differences of degree and form between the mineral realm and the thinking person. Man's characteristic privilege is that the bond he accepts is not physical but moral; this is, social. He is governed not by a material environment brutally imposed on him, but by a conscience superior to his own, the superiority of which he feels. Because the greater part of his existence transcends the body, he escapes the body's yoke, but is subject to that of society.
>
> Emile Durkheim, *Suicide: A Study in Sociology* (trans. J.A. Spaulding and G. Simpson). New York: Free Press, 1952.

How Do We Live with Other People?

> What matters to people is how they should live with other people. The great questions of social life are "Who am I?" (To what kind of a group do I belong) and "What should I do?" (Are there many or few prescriptions I am expected to obey?). Groups are strong or weak according to whether they have boundaries separating them from others. Decisions are taken either for the group as a whole (strong boundaries) or for individuals or families (weak boundaries). Prescriptions are few or many indicating the individual internalizes a large or a small number of behavioral norms to which he or she is bound. By combining boundaries with prescriptions...the most general answers to the questions of social life can be combined to form four different political cultures.

Fig. 3.16 Georg Simmel

SIMMEL

Aaron Wildavsky. "Conditions for a Pluralist Democracy or Cultural Pluralism means More Than One Political Culture in a Country." Unpublished manuscript. 1982.

Grid and Group Theory

The variability of an individual's involvement in social life can be adequately captured by two dimensions of sociality: group and grid. *Group* refers to the extent to which an individual is incorporated into bounded units. The greater the incorporation, the more individual choice is subject to group determination. *Grid* denotes the degree to which an individual's life is circumscribed by externally imposed prescriptions. The more binding and extensive the scope of the prescriptions, the less of life that is open to individual negotiation.

Michael Thompson, Richard Ellis, and Aaron Wildavsky. *Cultural Theory*. Boulder, CO: Westview. 1990 (Fig. 3.16).

On Poverty

The fact that someone is poor does not mean that he belongs to the specific social category of the "poor."….It is only from the moment that [the poor] are assisted…that they become part of a group characterized by poverty. The group does not remain united by interaction among its members, but by the collective attitude which society as a whole adopts toward it…..Poverty cannot be defined in itself as a quantitative state, but only in terms of the social reaction resulting from a specific situation.... Poverty is a unique sociological phenomenon: a number of individuals who, out of a purely individual fate, occupy a specific organic position within the whole; but this position is not determined by this fate and condition, but rather by the fact that others...attempt to correct this condition.

Georg Simmel, "The Poor." Trans. By Claire Jacobson in *Social Problems,* XIII, 2 (Fall, 1965).

Speech Codes and the Socialization of Children

I shall argue that forms of socialization orient the child towards speech codes which control access to relatively context-tied or relatively context-independent meanings. Thus I shall argue that elaborated codes orient their users towards universalistic meanings, whereas restricted codes orient, sensitize, their users to particularistic meanings: that the linguistic-realization of the two orders are different, and so are the social relationships which realize them. Elaborated codes are less tied to a given or local structure and thus contain the potentiality of change in principles.

Basil Bernstein, "Social Class, Language and Socialization" in Pier Paolo Giglioli, Ed. *Language and social context.* Harmondsworth, England: Penguin. 1972.

Collective Representations

Collective representations are the result of an immense co-operation, which stretches out not only into space but into time as well; to make them, a multitude of minds have associated, united, and combined their ideas and sentiments; for them, long generations have accumulated their experience and their knowledge. A special intellectual activity is therefore concentrated in them which is infinitely richer and complexer than that of the individual.

Emile Durkheim. *The Elementary Forms of Religious Life.* New York: Free Press. 1965.

Suicide

But when society is disturbed by some painful crisis or by beneficent but abrupt transitions, it is momentarily incapable of exercising this influence; thence come the sudden rises in the curve of suicide....Appetites, not being controlled by a public opinion, become disoriented, no longer recognize the limits proper to them....At the very moment when traditional rules have lost their authority, the richer prize offered these appetites stimulates them and makes them more exigent and impatient of control. The state of de-regulation or anomy is thus further heightened by passions being less disciplined, precisely when they need more disciplining.

Emile Durkheim, *Suicide: A Study in Sociology* (trans. J.A Spaulding and G. Simpson). 1952. New York, NY: Free Press.

Slavery

Amid all crouched the freed slave, bewildered between friend and foe. He had emerged from slavery,—not the worst slavery in the world, not a slavery that made all life unbearable, rather a slavery that had here and there something of kindliness, fidelity, and happiness,—but withal slavery, which, so far as human aspiration and desert were concerned, classed the black man and the ox together. And the Negro knew full well that, whatever their deeper convictions may have been, Southern men had fought with desperate energy to perpetuate this slavery under which the black masses, with half-articulate thought, had writhed and shivered.

W.E.B. Du Bois, *The Souls of Black Folk*. New York, NY: Dover Books. 1994.

The Cog in the Machine

The individual has become a mere cog in an enormous organization of things and powers which tear from his hands all progress, spirituality, and value in order to transform them from their subjective form into the form of a purely objective life. It needs merely to be pointed out that the metropolis is the genuine arena of this culture which outgrows all personal life. Here in buildings and educational institutions, in the wonders and comforts of space-conquering technology, in the formations of community life, and in the visible institutions of the state, is offered such an overwhelming fullness of crystallized and impersonalized spirit that the personality, so to speak, cannot maintain itself under its impact.

Georg Simmel, *The Metropolis and Mental Life*. Quoted in David Frisby and Mike Featherstone, (eds.) *Simmel on Culture*. Page 184. Taken from Hans Gerth (trans.) Kurt H. Wolff (ed.), *The Sociology of Georg Simmel,* Glencoe: Free Press, 1950, pp. 409–24.

The Representation of African Americans in the Media

If we compare the relative progress African Americans have made in education and employment to the struggle to gain control over how we are represented, particularly in the mass media, we see that there has been little change in the area of representation. Opening a magazine or book, turning on the television set, watching a film, or looking at photographs in public spaces, we are most likely to see the images of black people that reinforce and reinscribe white supremacy. Those images may be constructed by white people who have not divested of racism or by people of color/black people who may see the world through the lens of white supremacy—internalized racism.

bell hooks. *Black Looks: Race and Representation*. Boston: South End Press. 1992

The Recited Society

We now live in a "recited" society that constantly circulates narratives and stories through the medium of mass communication. In the post-truth world, the consent of the audience, the difference between that explosion of messages that char-

Fig. 3.17 Michel de Certeau

acterizes modernity is no longer stamped with the "authority" of their authors. De Certeau aptly describes the way in which old religious forms of authority have been supplanted by the plurality of narratives that empower the reader, rather than the writer....The central paradox of modernity identified by...de Certeau is that the more information that is produced by the power bloc, the less it is able to govern the various interpretations made of it by socially situated subjects

Nick Stevenson, *Understanding Media Cultures: Social Theory and Mass Communication*. London: Sage. 1985 (Fig. 3.17).

The Way People Use the Media

Many, often remarkable, works have sought to study the representations of a society, on the one hand, and its modes of behavior, on the other. Building on our knowledge of these social phenomena, it seems both possible and necessary to determine the *use* to which they are put by groups or individuals. For example, the analysis of the images broadcast by television (representation) and of the time spent watching television (behavior) should be complemented by a study of what the cultural consumer "makes" or "does" during this time with these images. The same goes for the use of urban space, the products purchased in the supermarket, the stories and legends distributed by the newspapers, and so on.

Michel de Certeau. *The Practice of Everyday Lie*. Trans. Steven Rendall. Berkeley, CA: University of California Press. 1984.

Behavior and Society

To understand individual experience one must study the social norms which make it possible.... Saussure, Freud, and Durkheim thus reverse the perspective which makes society the result of individual behavior and insist that behavior is made possible by collective social systems individuals have assimilated, consciously or unconsciously.

Jonathan Culler, *Ferdinand de Saussure*. (Revised edition). Ithaca, New York: Cornell University Press. 1986.

Ideology Is Everywhere

Contemporary criticism has forced students and teachers to see that there are no innocent texts, that all artifacts of established culture and society are laden with meaning, values, biases, and messages. There is no pure entertainment that does not contain representations—often extremely prejudicial—of class, gender, race, sexuality, and myriad social categories and groupings. Cultural texts are saturated with social meanings, they generate political effects, reproducing or opposing governing, social institutions and relations of domination and subordination. Culture can also embody specific political discourses—liberal, conservative, oppositional or mixed, advancing competing political positions on issues such as the family and sexuality, masculinity or femininity, or violence and war....Culture in today's societies thus constitutes a set of discourses, stories, images, spectacles, and varying cultural forms and practices that generate meaning, identities, and political effects. Culture includes artifacts such as newspapers, television programs, movies, and popular music, but also practices like shopping, watching sports events, going to a club, or hanging out at the local coffee shop. Culture is ordinary, a familiar part of everyday life, yet special cultural artifacts are extraordinary, helping people to see and understand things they've never quite perceived, like certain novels or films that change your view of the world.

Douglas M. Kellner and Meenakshi Gigi Durham,
"Adventures in Media and Cultural Studies: Introducing Key Works." in *Media and Cultural Studies: KeyWorks*. 2001.

Now that I have provided some insights and key statements about the four "pillars" of cultural studies, we are prepared to move on to my next chapter, which discusses media and everyday life.

REFERENCES

Adorno, Theodor W. 1948. *Philosophy of modern music*. New York: Seabury.
Barthes, Roland. 1972. (A. Lavers, trans.) *Mythologies*. New York, NY: Hill & Wang.
Bourdieu, Pierre. 1993. *Sociology in question*. London: Sage.
Brenner, Charles. 1974. *An elementary textbook of psychoanalysis*. Garden City, NY: Doubleday.

Chandler, Daniel. 2002. *Semiotics: The basics.* 3rd ed. Routledge.
Coser, Lewis. 1971. *Masters of sociological thought.* New York: Harcourt Brace Jovanovich.
Culler, Jonathan. 1986. *Ferdinand de Saussure* (Revised edition). Ithaca, New York: Cornell University Press.
de Certeau, Michel. 1984. *The practice of everyday life.* Berkeley, CA: University of California Press.
de Saussure, Ferdinand. 1966. *Course in general linguistics.* New York, NY: McGraw-Hill.
Durkheim, Emile. 1952. *Suicide: A study in sociology* (trans. J. A. Spaulding and G. Simpson). New York: Free Press, 1952.
———. 1965. *The elementary forms of the religious life.* New York, NY: Free Press.
Eco, Umberto. 1976. *A theory of semiotics.* Bloomington: Indiana University Press.
Featherstone. (ed.) 1950. *Simmel on culture*, p. 184. Taken from Hans Gerth (trans.) In Kurt H. Wolff (ed.), *The sociology of Georg Simmel*, Glencoe: Free Press, pp. 409–424.
Freud, Sigmund. 1924. *A general introduction to psycho-analysis.* New York: Washington Square Press.
Gottdiener, Mark. 1997. *The theming of America: Dreams, visions, and commercial spaces.* Boulder, CO: Westview.
Jensen, Joli. 1990. *Redeeming modernity: Contradictions in media criticism.* London: Sage.
Lazere, Donald. 1977. Mass culture, political consciousness, and English studies. *College English* 38: 755–756.
Lefebvre, Henri. 1971. *Everyday life in the modern world.* New York: Harper & Row.
Lenin, Vladimir. 1932. *State and revolution.* New York: International Publishers.
MacCannell, Dean. 1976. *The tourist: A new theory of the leisure class.* New York: Schocken Books.
Marx, Karl. 1964. *Selected writings in sociology and social philosophy* (T.B. Bottomore & M. Rubel, eds. T.B. Bottomore, Trans.). New York: McGraw-Hill.
Mitchell, Stephen A., and Margaret J. Black. 1996. *Freud and beyond: A history of modern psychoanalytic thought.* New York: Basic Books.
Pines, Maya. 1982, October 13. *How they know what you mean.* San Francisco: Chronicle.
Rieff, Philip, ed. 1963. *Freud: Character and culture.* New York, NY: Collier Books.
Sebeok, T.S., ed. 1977. *A perfusion of signs.* Bloomington: Indiana University Press.
Simmel, Georg. 1950. *The metropolis and mental life.* Quoted in David Frisby and Mike Thompson, Michael, Ellis, Richard, and Wildavsky, Aaron (1990). *Cultural theory.* Boulder, CO: Westview.

CHAPTER 4

Media and Everyday Life

Chapter Objectives The chapter offers a timeline on the Internet from 1939 to the present, showing when important technical achievements and applications took place. This is followed by a discussion of the amount of time people spend with traditional and digital media, which suggests that media occupy much of our time. The debate over media effects is dealt with along with an examination of social media, Facebook, and its impact upon people's psyches. Then, there is a treatment of uses and gratification theory, narratives, genres, and grid-group theory which is used to understand people's media preferences. The ideas of a French sociologist Pierre Bourdieu and the work of the Canadian media theorist Marshall McLuhan on electronic and print media and hot and cold media are discussed.

Keywords Internet • Media effect • Social media • Facebook • Uses and gratification theory • Narratives genres • Hot and cold media

> In contradistinction to the teleological, absolute, and single-minded Romantic narrative of "grand amour," the affair is a cultural form that attempts to immobilize and repeat, compulsively, the primordial experience of "novelty." During the Victorian era, people chose from a very narrow pool of available partners and often felt compelled to marry their first suitor. The contemporary affair, by contrast, presupposes variety and freedom to choose. This "shop--and--choose" outlook is due to a much wider pool of available partners and to the fact that a marketplace viewpoint—the belief that one should commit oneself after a long process of information gathering—has pervaded romantic practices…The affair can be viewed as a postmodern expression of *intensities* or experiences of pure sensations, desire, pleasures, non-mediated by reason, language, or a master narrative of self.

> Eva Illouz, "The Lost Innocence of Love: Romance as a Postmodern Condition," in *Theory, Culture & Society*. Vol. 15, Numbers 3–4, 1998.

> Eclecticism is the degree zero of contemporary general culture: one listens to reggae, watches a western, eats McDonald's food for lunch and local cuisine for dinner, wears Paris perfume in Tokyo, and "retro" clothes in Hong Kong; knowledge is a matter for TV games. It is easy to find a public for eclectic works. By becoming kitsch, art panders to the confusion which reigns in the "taste" of patrons. Artists, gallery owners, critics and the public wallow together in the "anything goes," and the epoch is one of slackening.

> Jean-François Lyotard, *The Postmodern Condition: A Report on Knowledge*. Minneapolis: University of Minnesota Press. 1984.

> The ingredients of the postmodern self are given in three key cultural identities, those derived from the performances that define gender, social class, race, and ethnicity…These cultural identities are filtered through the personal troubles and the emotional experiences that flow from the individual's interactions with everyday life. These existential troubles look back to the dominant cultural themes of the postmodern era, including the cult of Eros, and its idealized conceptions of love and intimacy.

> Norman Denzin. *Images of Postmodern Society: Social Theory and Contemporary Cinema*. London: Sage Publications. 1991.

It may be more correct to write that media *are* everyday life rather than writing about media *and* everyday life, since so much of our everyday lives is spent with media, of one kind or another. I begin this investigation of media and everyday life with a timeline showing how media technology and the Internet have evolved and then discuss how much media we use in a typical day.

Timeline on the Internet

There are many different timelines available on the Internet, some of which are long and detailed and others that are short and lack detail. I've taken material from various ones and created the timeline that follows. I've shown very important ones in boldface.

1939	First modern computer designed at Iowa State University.
1951	**UNIVAC, first civilian computer created.**
1969	ARPA (Advanced Research Projects Agency) connects four major US universities in December.
1972	**Pong, the first video game created.**
1972	**Electronic mail** was introduced by Ray Tomlinson who uses the @ to distinguish between the sender's name and network name in the email address.
1973	Transmission Control Protocol/Internet Protocol (TCP/IP).
1978	**Cellular phone service starts.**
1982	**The word "Internet" is first used.**
1984	**Domain Name System (DNS) created. Network addresses identified by extensions such as .com, .org, and .edu.**
1984	Writer William Gibson coins the term "cyberspace" created by writer William Gibson.
1984	**Apple Macintosh computer introduced.**
1983	TCP/IP becomes standard. FTP (File Transfer Protocol) developed so users can download files from a different computer.
1985	America Online, debuts, offers email, electronic bulletin boards, news, and other information.
1988	Internet Worm virus shuts down about 10% of the world's Internet servers.
1989	Tim Berners-Lee of CERN (European Laboratory for Particle Physics) develops the World Wide Web, based on hypertext, for distributing information on the Internet. The Web can now be accessed by a graphical user interface.
1991	Gopher interface is created at the University of Minnesota.
1993	HTML develops, the Internet opens to commercial use.
1993	Marc Andreessen develops Mosaic at the National Center for Supercomputing Applications (NCSA).
1994	The White House launches its website, www.whitehouse.gov.
1994	Internet vocabulary adds the term "spamming."
1994	Navigator browser and Netscape Communication created by Marc Andreessen and Jim Clark.
1994	**Amazon.com launched by Jeff Bezos.**
1995	CompuServe, America Online, and Prodigy started.
1995	Sun Microsystems releases the Internet programming language called Java.

1995 **First digital phones.**
1997 The term "weblog" is coined, becomes "blog."
1997 **Netflix created.**
1998 **Google opens its first office, in California.**
1999 MySpace.com is launched.
2000 Viruses now become a problem.
2001 **Birth of Wikipedia.**
2003 Spam becomes a big problem.
2003 **Apple Computer creates Apple iTunes Music Store.**
2004 **Facebook is created.**
2004 **Gmail is created.**
2005 **YouTube.com** is launched.
2006 There are more than 92 million websites online.
2006 **Twitter microblogging application invented.**
2007 Online game, World of Warcraft, has more than 9 million subscribers worldwide.
2007 **Apple iPhone introduced.**
2010 **Apple iPad introduced.**
2010 **Pinterest introduced.**
2011 Sixteen billion indexed Web pages on the Internet.
2011 **Snapchat launched.**
2012 Google Glass, wearable computers become popular.
2012 **Instagram launched.**
2012 Advanced Smart Watches.
2014 Oculus Virtual Reality Headphone.
2014 "Right to be forgotten" ruling in Europe.
2015 **Apple Smart Watch,**
2017 **TikTok launched,**

This timeline gives you a useful overview of how electronic media have evolved since 1939 when a prototype of the modern computer was created at Iowa State University.

A report in eMarketer offers some statistics on our time spent with various media in 2013 (Table 4.1):

We used to spend 11 h a day with media. By 2020, we had increased our media exposure to more than 13 h a day with them, with a large increase in the time we spent with digital media (Table 4.2).

In 2020, US adults increased their time spent with media by nearly an hour per day—58 minutes—to a new high average of 13 hours, 21 minutes (13:21). Last year, time spent with most media formats and devices grew, with digital media specifically seeing huge gains. Some traditional media formats like TV and print newspapers saw growth for the first time in years, but others fell slightly.
https://www.emarketer.com/content/us-time-spent-with-media-2021

Table 4.1 Time spent with electronic media in 2013

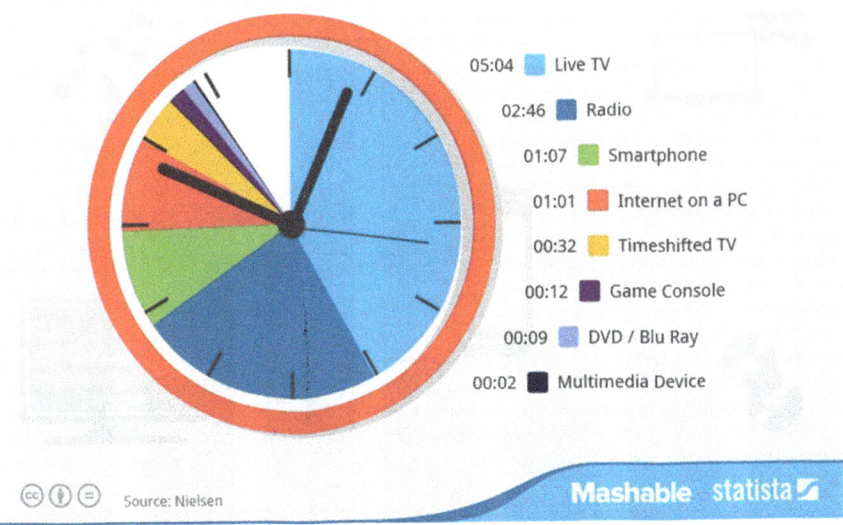

TIME SPENT WITH TRADITIONAL VS DIGITAL MEDIA

The eMarketer report (accessed 10/30/2021) shows how digital media is growing substantially and has grown from 49 percent of time spent with media in 2017 to a projected 63.7 percent of the time for 2023.

According to eMarketer, in 2020:

> US adults spent an average of 13:21 per day with media in 2020, up from the 12:23 spent per day in 2019. This growth was entirely due to an increase in time spent with digital media, which grew from 6:49 in 2019 to 7:50 in 2020. Time spent with digital media is expected to continue to increase, albeit at a slower pace, reaching 7:59 per day in 2021 and 8:09 in 2022.
> https://www.marketingcharts.com/industries/media-and-entertainment-117666

If we spend 13 h a day with media, and almost 8 h of those hours with digital media, it means media is with us just about all the time. We spend around 8 min a day with printed on paper newspapers and a total of 20 min a day reading printed on paper matter such as newspapers, magazines, and books but we may read newspaper and magazine articles on our cellphones:

> **The average daily time spent reading by individuals in the United States in 2020 amounted to 0.34 hours or 20.4 minutes. Adults over the age of 65 were the most avid readers, and those aged 75 or above spent almost an hour reading each day. (July 26, 2021.)**

Table 4.2 Time spent with traditional vs. digital media in US

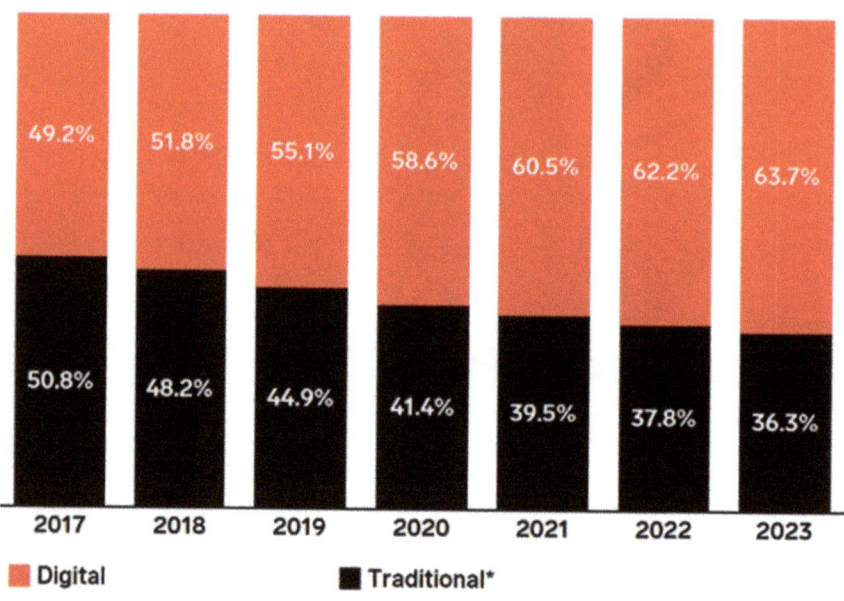

https://www.google.com/search?q=hours+spent+reading+books+in+America

We spent less time with television, down from 313 min a day (about 5 h) to 253 min a day (about 4 h). Our time on the Internet has grown from 127 min a day (about 2 h) in 2012 to 301 min a day (about 5 h), and it is projected that we will be spending 8 h a day on digital media in a few years (Table 4.3).

This chart is a Zenith media forecast taken from the Internet.

We live, these statistics suggest, media-saturated lives, and our everyday lives are defined, in many respects, by the choices we make in what media to consume.

The media carry texts of all kinds, so we must keep in mind that the kind of programs we watch, films we see, or books we read and what we follow on the

Table 4.3 Minutes spent per person per medium

Daily minutes consumed per person, per medium							
	Newspapers	Magazines	Television	Radio	Internet	(Desktop)	(Mobile)
2012	21.0	22.5	313.8	120.0	127.2	(67.7)	(59.5)
2013	21.3	21.3	305.8	116.0	141.1	(67.3)	(73.8)
2014	19.6	19.6	297.8	111.0	154.9	(66.9)	(88.1)
2015	17.0	18.6	289.0	109.0	180.0	(56.0)	(124.0)
2016	15.0	17.6	287.4	104.5	189.0	(53.0)	(136.0)
2017	14.0	16.5	282.1	102.0	217.0	(53.0)	(164.0)
2018	12.4	15.2	270.4	102.0	236.8	(52.0)	(190.0)
2019	11.0	14.0	263.6	100.0	259.2	(51.0)	(208.2)
2020	9.5	12.7	258.3	100.0	281.1	(50.0)	(231.1)
2021	8.0	12.0	253.2	99.0	301.9	(50.0)	(251.9)
Source: Zenith Media Consumption Forecasts, Fifth Edition, June 2019.							

Internet are genre-based forms of culture, or, in many cases, popular culture such as romance novels, news programs, action-adventure shows, sporting events, and so on.

FOCAL POINTS FOR THE STUDY OF MEDIA

There are, I suggest, five focal points that we can keep in mind when dealing with the media. The chart that follows is taken from my book *Media and Communication Research Methods,* 5th edition (Fig. 4.1).

This model shows that all the focal points are connected and suggests that many factors play a role in the creation and consumption of mediated texts. We can focus our attention on the artist, a medium, or the media that carries the text, on the text itself, on the audience of the text, and on the society or country where the text was created. Or we can deal with one or two or more of the focal points, depending upon our interests.

For example, let's consider Stan Lee's Marvel Comics and the films made based on Lee's characters.

> We can focus on **Lee** and write a biographical analysis of Lee and his creations.
> We can focus on the **texts:** his comic books and the films made from Lee's characters.
> We can focus on the **media** that Lee used: comic books and also on the films that were made based on characters in Marvel Comics.
> We can study the **audiences** for Marvel Comics and the films made with characters in Marvel comics.
> We can study the impact of Marvel Comics and Marvel films on **American** character and culture.

Fig. 4.1 Focal points in studying media

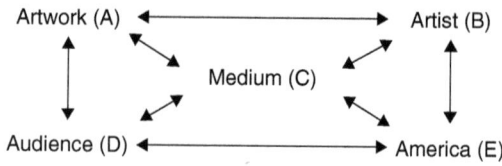

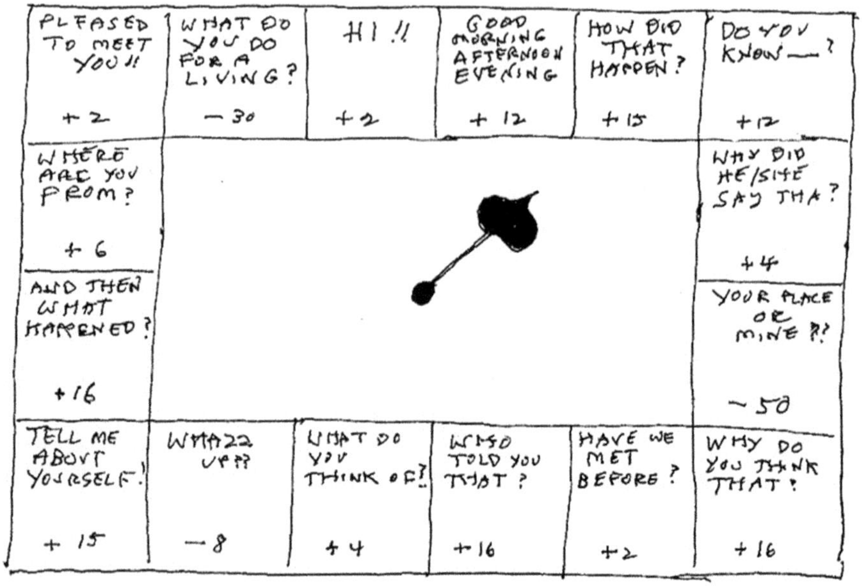

Fig. 4.2 The Game of Love

A considerable amount of research into the media deals with the audiences of texts and is quantitative, while many other researchers focus upon texts and their impact upon audiences and what they reflect about the societies in which the texts are found. This is described as qualitative research, and sometimes we find mixtures with both kinds of research in an article or book? (Fig. 4.2)

Case Study: Metaphor and "All in the Game"

In 1951, a popular song titled "All in the Game" became popular. One of its lines went, "All in the wonderful game called love," which suggested that love *is* a game, a metaphor that has interesting and important implications. If love is a game, that means love has many of the characteristics of games which involves the following:

Games are won and lost.
What does it mean to "lose" in the game of love?
People often use deception when playing games.
Does this mean people often deceive each other in love relationships?
People cheat in games.
How do people cheat in the game of love?
Games always end.
Does that mean love always ends?
Games always have rules.
What are the rules in the game of love? What if people don't obey the rules?
Games are not serious.
Does that mean we stop loving whenever we want because games and love are trivial?
We often play games more than once.
Does this mean that love relationships are bound to end and to be "replayed" with others?

My point is that if people think of love as a game, that will affect their ideas about what love is and what it means to have a love relationship, generally in very negative ways. A weaker form of metaphor, a simile, would argue that love is like a game, and would also have the same negative implications. And it is the implications of metaphors and similes that are important.

We must realize that metaphor plays an important role in our everyday lives. As George Lakoff and Mark Johnson explain in their book *Metaphors We Live By* (1980, p. 3):

> Metaphor is for most people a device of the poetic imagination and the rhetorical flourish—a matter of extraordinary rather than ordinary language. Moreover, metaphor is typically viewed as a characteristic of language alone, a matter of words rather than thought or action. For this reason, most people think they can get along perfectly well without metaphor. We have found, on the contrary, that metaphor is pervasive in everyday life, not just in language but in thought and action. Our ordinary conceptual system, in terms of which we both think and act, is fundamentally metaphoric in nature. The concepts that govern our thought are not just matters of the intellect. They also govern our everyday functioning, down to the most mundane details. Our concepts structure what we perceive, how we get around in the world, and how we relate to other people. Our conceptual system thus plays a central role in defining our everyday realities. If we are right in suggesting that our conceptual system is largely metaphorical, what we experience and what we do every day is very much a matter of metaphor.
>
> The concepts that govern our thoughts are not just matters of the intellect. They also govern our everyday functioning, down to the most mundane details. Our concepts structure what we perceive, how we get around in the world, and how we relate to other people. Our conceptual system thus plays a central role in defining our everyday realities.

Metaphor, then, is much more commonly used than we imagine and plays an important role "in defining our everyday realities."

I dealt with the primary methods of textual analysis in the last chapter, where I discussed the cultural studies approach to media along with my brief introductions to semiotic theory, psychoanalytic theory, Marxist criticism, and sociological analysis. I deal with an important aspect of media studies in my discussion of media effects. If media effects are trivial, it doesn't matter if we spend 13 h a day with media, but if they are important, and I believe that is the case, then our daily media consumption is of great significance.

Media Effects

In the 1980s, there was a great deal of debate among media scholars about the effects of media upon people. Some scholars argued that the media have long-lasting and powerful effects upon audiences, while others argued that the media effects were short-lasting and relatively unimportant. Wikipedia offers an overview of this matter:

> Starting in the 1930s, the second phase of media effects studies instituted the importance of empirical research while introducing the complex nature of media effects due to the idiosyncratic nature of individuals in an audience.[11] The Payne Fund studies, conducted in the United States during this period, focused on the effect of media on young people. Many other separate studies focused on persuasion effects studies, or the possibilities and usage of planned persuasion in film and other media. Hovland et al. (1949) conducted a series of experimental studies to evaluate the effects of using films to indoctrinate American military recruits.[15] Paul Lazarsfeld (1944) and his colleagues' effectiveness studies of democratic election campaigns launched political campaign effect studies.[16]
>
> Researchers uncovered mounting empirical evidence of the idiosyncratic nature of media effects on individuals and audiences, identifying numerous intervening variables such as demographic attributes, social psychological factors, and different media use behaviors. With these new variables added to research, it was difficult to isolate media influence that resulted in any media effects to an audience's cognition, attitude, and behavior. As Berelson (1959) summed up in a widely quoted conclusion: "Some kinds of communication on some kinds of issues have brought to the attention of some kinds of people under some kinds of conditions have some kinds of effect."[17] Though the concept of an all-powerful mass media was diluted, this did not determine that the media lacked influence or effect. Instead, the pre-existing structure of social relationships and cultural contexts were believed to primarily shape or change people's opinions, attitudes, and behaviors, and media merely function within these established processes. This complexity had a dampening effect upon media effects studies.[14]
>
> https://en.wikipedia.org/wiki/Influence_of_mass_media

William J. McGuire, a professor of psychology at Yale University, wrote an article in 1991, "Who's Afraid of the Big Bad Media?" in which he argued that we cannot prove that the media have a significant impact upon people. He concluded his article (found in Arthur Asa Berger, Ed., *Media USA: Process and Effect* (1988, p. 279):

> Although the general public and the diverse groups who are professionally involved with the media may be convinced that the mass media have vast direct impacts on the public, a considerable amount of empirical research on the topic has provided surprisingly little support for massive impact. Rather, the interim bottom line to which the existing research findings add up is that media effects can occasionally be directed statistically but are usually quite small in magnitude….For the present, a Scotch verdict of "Not Proven" seems indicated on the proposition that the mass media have vast direct impacts on the public exposed to them.

In his article, McGuire lists some reasons why researchers can believe in the notion of strong media impacts:

1. Methodological weaknesses may obscure effects.
2. Environmental conditions may obscure media impact.
3. Circumscribed effects may be missed in the search for general effects.
4. Effects may be confined to especially susceptible subpopulations.
5. Indirect effects may be missed in the search for direct effects.

These factors may explain why researchers were unable to document the powerful, long-lasting, and important effects of the media upon people. I would suggest that this notion that the media do not have a strong impact upon people no longer is the dominant position when it comes to the matter of media effects.

Social Media: Revelations about Facebook's Impact

We now have evidence of the impact of social media upon people in the revelations by Frances Haugen about research carried out by Facebook. In a "Morning Edition" program on National Public Radio, "Ex-Facebook employee Frances Haugen testifies before Senate panel," with Steve Inskeep and Shannon Bond, held on October 6, 2021, we read:

> BOND: Well, she focused in on Facebook's engagement-based algorithms. That's her area of expertise. You know, the way that works is, when you're on Facebook or Instagram, if a post gets a lot of interactions, comments, likes, it's spread more widely. It's featured more prominently, the idea being that keeps people interested in using the apps. But Haugen cited Facebook's own research showing that focusing on engagement also tends to amp up the most sensational and extreme posts. So, for example, people might be looking for healthy recipes, but then they start seeing posts about anorexia. She says it's even fueling ethnic violence in places like Ethiopia. And she says Facebook needs to be pressured to fix it.

What we learn from Haugen is that Facebook has had a negative impact on American politics, generating extremist beliefs, and upon the psyches of people who use it.

Social Media: Facebook and the Net Effect

David Brunskill, an Australian psychiatrist, wrote an important article "Social Media, Social Avatars and the Psyche: Is Facebook Good for Us" about Facebook's impact on our lives. In his article, he writes (Quoted in Arthur Asa Berger, *Media and Communication Research Methods,* 5th Ed. (2020, p. 43):

> …Five psychological forces (Grandiosity, Narcissism, Darkness, Regression and Impulsivity) vie to assert themselves as the material from which the e-personality is built and that they—in a twenty-first century confirmation of the Freudian id—cause a transformation (and fracture) of personality, known as the Net Effect.

Brunskill adds that Facebook may be addictive and that while it can be used for positive purposes, it also can be used for bullying people and spreading lies and hateful material. We should recognize that many people spend a great deal of time on Facebook as the following, taken from the Internet on 10/21/2021, indicates:

> Last year, driven in no small part by the pandemic, Americans spent more than an average 1300 hours on social media according to a new study from Uswitch. Facebook led the way, where Americans spent an average 58 minutes a day on the app – or 325 hours a year.
> https://www.google.com/search?sxsrf=AOaemvJwFjppyvuup56i6m7Hvi5w NsK7eQ:1635692277322&q=amount+of+time+people+in+US+spend+on+Fac ebook&spell=1&sa=X&ved=2ahUKEwi90prJ9PTzAhWEaDABHeeaBqcQBSg AegQIARAx&biw=1111&bih=747&dpr=1

If Americans spend 13 h a day with media, and if the media are powerful, we must conclude that the media play an important role in our everyday lives and matters such as our mental health, political beliefs, and consumer preferences.

Social Media: The Internet and Depression

When it comes to the Internet, there are reasons to suggest that while it has brought us many useful things, like free universities, search engines, Skype, and Zoom, the Internet also has had a negative impact on our well-being.

In his book, *On the Internet* (2nd edition), Herbert L. Dreyfus (2009), a philosophy professor at the University of California in Berkeley, discusses research in his book about some negative effects of the Internet. He quotes from an article by R. Kraut et al. who authored an article "Internet Paradox: A Social Technology that Reduces Social Involvement and Psychological Well-Being" (*American Psychologist,* 1998, vol. 53, no. 9, pp. 1017–31):

The research examined the social and psychological impact of the Internet on 169 people in seventy-three households during their first one or two years online....In this sample, the Internet was used extensively for communication. Nonetheless, the greater use of the Internet was associated with declines in participants' communication with family members in the household, declines in the size of their social circle, and increases in depression and loneliness....On-line friendships are likely to be more limited than friendships supported by physical proximity....Because on-line friends are not embedded in the same day-to-day environment, they will be less likely to understand the context for conversation, making discussion more difficult and rendering support less applicable. Even strong ties maintained at a distance through electronic communication are likely to be different in kind and perhaps diminished in strength compared with strong ties supported by physical proximity. The interpersonal communication applications currently prevalent on the Internet are either neutral toward strong ties or tend to undercut them rather than promote them.

The Internet can be described as a two-edged sword, which has both positive and negative features. In recent years, we have recognized that the Internet, and applications like Facebook and TikTok, may have a much more negative impact on people who use them than we had imagined.

In this chapter, so far, I have discussed the five focal points we can consider in studying the media and media effects. On the latter topic, I have argued that the media have long-lasting and powerful effects and used Facebook and the Internet as an example of how the media can affect us as individuals and impact upon our societies. Consider the impact that Facebook, Twitter, and other social media have had on our politics, our attitudes about wearing masks and getting vaccinated, and many other topics where falsehoods, misinformation, and other socially destructive misinformation have been spread.

Now I will address an important question: how do people decide what programs to watch on television, listen to on the radio, choose books, magazines, and newspapers to read, and make media choices in general.

USES AND GRATIFICATIONS THEORY: A DIFFERENT APPROACH TO MEDIA RESEARCH

The focus in uses and gratifications theory is on the ways people use media and the various gratifications media offer to people. Elihu Katz, Jay G. Blumler, and Michael Gurevitch (1979) mention some early works on the subject:

> Herzog (1942) on quiz programs and the gratifications derived from listening to soap operas; Suchman (1942) on the motives for getting interested in serious music on radio; Wolfe and Fiske (1949) on the development of children's interest in comics; Berelson (1949) on the functions of newspaper reading; and so on.
>
> These investigations all led to a list of functions served either by some specific kind of text or by some medium. Some of the functions involved matching one's wits against others, obtaining advice for daily living, providing a framework for

one's day, preparing oneself for the demands of upward mobility, or being reassured about the dignity and usefulness of one's role.

The material that follows is informed by several different sources. It is difficult to decide, in some cases, whether a given reason people use the media involves uses, gratifications, needs, or desires, but they are all are relatively similar in what they do. I assume this list of some of the most important uses and gratifications of media usage is self-explanatory. This list is adapted from Arthur Asa Berger, *Media Analysis Techniques*. 6th Ed. (2019:170–171):

1. To be amused and entertained
2. To see authority figures exalted or deflated
3. To experience the beautiful
4. To share experiences with others
5. To satisfy curiosity and be informed
6. To identify with the deity and the divine plan
7. To find distraction and diversion
8. To experience empathy
9. To experience, in a guilt-free situation, extreme emotions
10. To find models to imitate
11. To gain identity
12. To gain information about the world
13. To reinforce belief in justice
14. To reinforce belief in romantic love
15. To reinforce belief in magic, the marvelous, and the miraculous
16. To see others make mistakes
17. To see order imposed on the world
18. To participate vicariously in history
19. To be purged of unpleasant emotions
20. To obtain outlets for sexual drives in a guilt-free context
21. To explore taboo subjects with impunity
22. To experience the ugly
23. To affirm moral, spiritual, and cultural values
24. To see villains in action

As this list suggests, the mass-mediated texts provide a significant number of gratifications to people which helps explain why they are so popular. But why do some people choose to watch particular programs and particular genres (sports, cop shows, news) rather than others (operas, quiz shows, documentaries)?

Genres and the Media

When we watch television, go to the movies, read a book, or wander around the Internet, the texts we choose are generally based on our like or dislike of certain genres, a French term that means "kind" or "category." People essentially decide what genres they like and what texts in those genres to read or watch.

As Douglas Kellner explains in *Television Images, Codes and Messages* (1980, Vol. 7, No. 4):

> A genre consists of a coded set of formulas and conventions which indicate a culturally accepted way of organizing material into distinct patterns. Once established, genres dictate the basic conditions of cultural production and reception. For example, crime dramas invariably have a violent crime, a search for its perpetrators, and often a chase, fight, or bloody elimination of the criminal, communicating the message "crime does not pay." The audience comes to expect these predictable pleasures and a crime drama "code" develops, enshrined in production and studio texts and practices.

To further complicate matters, many genres have sub-genres. Thus, for example, the detective genre has three sub-genres: the classical detective story with a detective who uses his or her brains (Sherlock Holmes), the tough guy detective story with a hero who is smart but also who is good with his fists (Sam Spade), and the procedural detective story (CSI) about police laboratories and teams of police fighting crime.

Generally, we divide books into two major genres: fiction and non-fiction. When it comes to popular fiction, certain genres are particularly important: romance novels, mysteries, science fiction stories, horror stories, spy stories, westerns, comic novels, and so on. Popular fiction tends to be highly formulaic, while elite literature, such as the novels of James Joyce, is not. Below I offer a chart that I constructed which shows the formulaic elements in three important genres (Table 4.4).

A search on Google (accessed 11/1/2021) reveals that the most popular fiction genres are:

Table 4.4 Formulas in popular literature genres

Genre	*Western*	*Science fiction*	*Spy*
Location	Edge of civ.	Space	World
Time	1800s	Future	Present
Hero	Cowboy	Spaceman	Secret agent
Heroine	Schoolmarm	Spacegal	Woman spy
Secondary chars	Townsfolk	Technicians	Other spies
Plot	Restore law	Repeal aliens	Find moles
Themes	Justice	Save humanity	Save free world
Costume	Cowboy hat	High-tech	Suit
Locomotion	Horse	Spaceship	Planes, fast cars
Weaponry	Six-gun	Ray gun	Pistol/silencer

Note: This table is adapted from one in Arthur Asa Berger, *Essentials of Mass Communication Theory*. 1995. Sage

1. *Romance/Erotica – $1.44 billion* – From the success of the Fifty Shades of Grey trilogy and the number of novels written by people like Danielle Steele, there's no surprise that romance and erotica are #1.
2. *Crime/Mystery* – $728.2 million – There's nothing like the thrill from a mystery novel. The suspense is intriguing enough that it keeps you on board. It's all about the build-up, the surprises, even the letdowns. Crime and mystery stories are so wild and fascinating, but also seem plausible.
3. *Religious/Inspirational* – $720 million – Things may be going great but you may need a little push. Everyone can use some inspiration. From how-to books, holy texts, and even memoirs, inspirational and religious texts.
4. *Science Fiction/Fantasy* – $590.2 million – Dragons, elves, witches, robots, the possibilities are endless. We love escaping into a fictional land. There's nothing that people can't achieve through magic or extraordinary circumstances in this genre.
5. *Horror – $79.6 million* – Horror has earned its place on this list. If you think of Stephen King and the ways his work has been adapted to screen, or old horrors like Dracula and Frankenstein, there are endless stories that people love.

https://bookadreport.com/book-market-overview-authors-statistics-facts/

There are also blendings in which you combine science fiction and horror or romance and crime mystery stories. These genres are popular because of the uses readers make of them and because of the gratifications they offer.

A Case Study: Gratifications from Romance Novels

Reading the Romance: Women, Patriarchy, and Popular Literature, by Janice Radway (1991), is a study of romance novel readers that began as an attempt to find out about the uses and gratifications that romance novels offer readers. Radway spent time with romance readers which led to her changing her study.

The book gradually became less an account of the way romances as texts were interpreted than a report on the way romance reading functioned as a form of behavior operated as a complex intervention in the ongoing social life of actual social subjects, women who saw themselves first as wives and mothers.

Radway offers some observations about the ability that individuals and groups of readers have to resist the power of those who control the media (1991, p. 222):

> If we can learn, then, to look at the ways in which various groups appropriate and use the mass-produced art of our culture, I suspect we may well begin to understand that although the ideological power of contemporary cultural forms is enormous, indeed sometimes even frightening, that power is not yet all-pervasive, totally vigilant, or complete. Interstices still exist within the social fabric where

opposition is carried on by people who are not satisfied by their place within it or by the restricted material and emotional rewards that accompany it.

By studying a group of romance novel readers, Radway learned that it is possible, and perhaps often the case, that people can learn how to resist the power of the mass media to shape their consciousness.

The Importance of Narratives

We must recognize that many of the texts to which we are attracted are narratives—that is, they are stories that have a linear and sequential structure in which one thing leads to another until the narrative concludes. Narratives tend to take place within a certain time. They tend to be linear, but in some cases, narratives jump around and move in various configurations. Yuri Lotman, a Russian semiotician, has argued that everything in a narrative is significant. As he explained in *The Structure of the Artistic Text* (1977, p. 17):

> The tendency to interpret everything in an artistic text as meaningful is so great that we rightfully consider nothing accidental in a work of art.

What this means is that everything plays a role in narratives, even though some elements in the narrative may seem irrelevant at first sight. Stories all have gaps in them and are full of holes since writers can't describe every thought and every idea a character might have and everything characters do. The role of readers is to fill in the gaps and make sense of things as best they can. This means that readers play an important role in interpreting what a story is all about and different readers get different things out of a given narrative. They use description, dialogue, and many other techniques to achieve their effects.

Narratives play an important role in our everyday lives. As Laurel Richardson explains in her article "Narrative and Sociology," *Journal of Contemporary Ethnology*, 19, 118, 1990):

> Narrative is the primary way through which humans organize their experiences into temporally meaningful episodes.... Narrative is both a mode of reasoning *and* a mode of representation. People can "apprehend" the world narratively and people can "tell" about the world narratively. According to Jerome Bruner...narrative reasoning is one of the two basic and universal human cognition modes. The other mode is the logico-scientific....The logico-scientific mode looks for universal truth conditions, whereas the narrative mode looks for particular connections between events. Explanation in the narrative mode is contextually embedded, whereas the logico-scientific explanation is extracted from spatial and temporal events. Both modes are "rational" ways of making meaning.

So narratives are not just mindless entertainments and, it can be argued, help shape the way we think about things and ourselves.

Grid-Group Theory: Media Preferences for Specific Texts

We have dealt with generalized choices people make about genres and subgenres they like but we have not identified why people like particular television programs, books, songs, games, and other kinds of mediated texts.

To answer this question, I will discuss the work of social anthropologist Mary Douglas and her work on grid-group theory. What Douglas argued was that people in modern societies belong to one of four lifestyles and that people's membership in a particular lifestyle is shaped by two forces: the strength of the boundaries of the groups to which they belong (weak or strong) and the number of rules and prescriptions to which they are subject (few or many).

In their book, *Cultural Theory*, written by Michael Thompson, Richard Ellis, and Aaron Wildavsky, we find an explanation of grid-group theory (1990, p. 5):

> Our theory has a specific point of departure: the Grid-Group typology proposed by Mary Douglas. She argues that the variability of an individual's involvement with social life can be adequately captured by two dimensions of sociality: group and grid. *Group* refers to the extent to which an individual is incorporated in bounded units. The greater the incorporation, the more the individual is subject to group determination. *Grid* denotes the degree to which an individual's life is circumscribed by externally imposed prescriptions. The more binding and extensive the scope of the prescriptions, the less of life that is open to individual negotiation.

Grid-group theory argues, then, is that our behavior is shaped by two different forces: one is the strength of the groups to which we belong (and the amount of control they have over us) and the other is the number of rules and prescriptions to which we are subject. The group boundaries can be very strong or relatively weak and the number of rules and prescriptions can be few in number or numerous. Thus, Catholic priests have strong group boundaries and many rules, while Reform rabbis have weak group boundaries and few rules.

Wildavsky (1982) explained why we form political cultures (a political form or version of lifestyles) or, outside of politics, what Mary Douglas describes as "lifestyles." As Wildavsky wrote in "Conditions for a Pluralist Democracy or Cultural Pluralism Means More Than One Political Culture in a Country" (quoted in A.A. Berger, 1990, p. 7):

> What matters to people is how they should live with other people. The great questions of social life are "Who am I?" (To what kind of a group do I belong?) and What should I do? (Are there many or few prescriptions I am expected to obey?). Groups are strong or weak according to whether they have boundaries separating them from others. Decisions are taken either for the group as a whole (strong boundaries) or for individuals or families (weak boundaries). Prescriptions are few or many indicating the individual internalizes a large or a small number of

Table 4.5 Lifestyle group boundaries and rules

Lifestyle	Group boundaries	Number of rules
Hierarchical elitist	Strong	Many and varied
Egalitarian	Strong	Few
Individualist	Weak	Few
Fatalist	Weak	Many and varied

behavioral norms to which he or she is bound. By combining boundaries with prescriptions... the most general answers to the questions of social life can be combined to form four different political cultures.

Different theorists have given these lifestyles different names, but the names all suggest what it is that generates the lifestyle. The names for the lifestyles I've used were used by Aaron Wildavsky in his work on political cultures; Mary Douglas had different names for egalitarians and fatalists: enclavists and isolates. We get a four-celled figure, with group boundaries that are strong or weak and rules and prescriptions that are few or numerous (Table 4.5).

Wildavsky explained how these groups are formed. He writes (quoted in A.A. Berger, 1990, p. 6):

> Strong groups with numerous prescriptions that vary with social roles combine to form hierarchical collectivism. Strong groups whose members follow few prescriptions form an egalitarian culture, a shared life of voluntary consent, without coercion or inequality. Competitive individualism joins few prescriptions with weak boundaries, thereby encouraging ever new combinations. When groups are weak and prescriptions strong, so that decisions are made for them by people on the outside, the controlled culture is fatalistic.

Douglas used the term "isolates" for Wildavsky's "fatalists" and "enclavists" for his "egalitarians," and Wildavsky changed the terms he used at times. The important thing is that each of these groups can be located in the figure relative to their relationship to the strength of group boundaries and the number of rules to which they are subject.

The important point for grid-group theorists is that our everyday lives and the decisions we make about all kinds of different things are shaped, to a considerable extent, by our grid-group affiliations or "lifestyles." In her seminal article "In Defence of Shopping," Douglas offers some insights into the nature of each lifestyle. Her article is found in Pasi Falk and Colin Campbell's *The Shopping Experience* (1977) and points out that an acceptance of one lifestyle involves a rejection of the three other lifestyles. In her article on shopping, Douglas offers an important insight about these four lifestyles (1977, p. 19):

> None of these four lifestyles (individualist, hierarchical, enclavist, isolated) is new to students of consumer behavior. What may be new and unacceptable is the point that these are the only four distinctive lifestyles to be taken into account,

and the other point, that each is set up in competition with the others. Mutual hostility is the force that accounts for their stability.

What is important about these groups, Douglas writes, is that they shape our choices in many areas. It is our cultural alignments that are the strongest predictors of our consumer preferences. When we are wandering around shopping centers or doing any shopping we are, without being aware of the full significance of what we are doing, actualizing the lifestyle to which we are attached and rejecting the kinds of choices made by members of other lifestyles. She writes (1997, p. 17):

> We have to make a radical shift away from thinking about consumption as a manifestation of individual choices. Culture itself is the result of a myriad of individual choices, not primarily between commodities but between kinds of relationships. The basic choice a rational individual has to make is the choice about what kind of society to live in. According to that choice, the rest follows. Artefacts are selected to demonstrate that choice. Food is eaten, clothes are worn, cinema, books, music, holidays, all the rest are choices that conform with the initial choice for a form of society.

When she writes the word "society" she is referring to lifestyles. Her thesis attacks those who argue that it is individual taste and preferences that shape our decision-making and consumer behavior. What seems to be individual taste, her argument suggests, is based on unconscious imperatives located in the lifestyle to which people belong and the rejection of other lifestyles.

According to her theory, cultural bias shapes our behavior. "Shopping," she writes, "is agonistic—a struggle not to define what one is, but what one is not," which means that shopping is, since we are rejecting the kinds of choices made by members of other lifestyles, ultimately an act of cultural defiance.

We can apply grid-group theory to our taste in popular culture texts. When we apply her theories to media texts, we are arguing that there are, in essence, four audiences and these audiences choose texts that support and reinforce their ideas and values.

Below I offer a chart, based on the four lifestyles and the media texts most in tune with each lifestyle. It is very difficult to figure out why people choose the songs they like to listen to, films they want to see, or books they want to read, but grid-group theory offers a way of understanding how our initial choice of a lifestyle affects our media preferences. I've left some topics blank for readers to determine what to choose (Table 4.6).

What this table reveals is that our lifestyles affect and shape our media preferences and also that our media preferences reveal our lifestyles. Our tastes, if Mary Douglas is correct, are shaped by unconscious imperatives located in our lifestyles.

If personal opinion and personal taste are illusions and are really socially determined, our media preferences move from being a matter of our

Table 4.6 Lifestyles and media preferences

Topic	Elitist	Individualist	Egalitarian	Fatalist
Songs	God Save The Queen	I Did It My Way	We Are The World	
TV shows	Elizabeth	Dynasty	The Equalizer	
Films	The Crown		Woodstock	
Magazines	*Architectural Digest*	*Money*	*Mother Jones*	
Books	*The Prince*	*Looking Out for Number One*	*I'm Okay, You're Okay*	*1984*
Sports	Polo	Tennis	Frisbee	Roller Derby
Games	Chess	Monopoly	New Games	Russian Roulette

psychological needs and interests to being socially determined. Perhaps, as Mary Douglas argues, by our choice of one of the four lifestyles or by other social matters like our socio-economic status or cultural capital, as Bourdieu would describe things.

His ideas on taste are discussed in a Wikipedia article on his ideas about taste:

> Bourdieu was a prolific author, producing hundreds of articles and three dozen books, nearly all of which are now available in English. His best-known book is *Distinction: A Social Critique of the Judgment of Taste* (1979), in which he argues that judgments of taste are related to social position, or more precisely, are themselves acts of social positioning. The argument is put forward by an original combination of social theory and data from quantitative surveys, photographs and interviews, in an attempt to reconcile difficulties such as how to understand the subject within objective structures. In the process, Bourdieu attempts to reconcile the influences of both external social structures and subjective experience on the individual.[i] The book would go on to be named "the sixth most important sociological work of the twentieth century" by the International Sociological Association (ISA).[6]
>
> Pierre Bourdieu's work emphasized how social classes, especially the ruling and intellectual classes, preserve their social privileges across generations despite the myth that contemporary post-industrial society boasts equality of opportunity and high social mobility, achieved through formal education.
> https://en.wikipedia.org/wiki/Pierre_Bourdieu

For Bourdieu, it would seem, as I explained earlier in the book, personal taste is an illusion, but that does not mean that taste is an illusion: there are other explanations for taste that are social, cultural, and economic in nature.

I have, to this point, discussed many of the focal points shown in my table—works of art (texts), audiences, authors, and America (or any society), but I have not dealt with media, per se.

Fig. 4.3 Marshall McLuhan

That is the subject of what follows and relies on the ideas of the Canadian media theorist Marshall McLuhan as expressed in his book *Understanding Media: The Extensions of Man*, published in 1965, and many other works (Fig. 4.3).

Marshall McLuhan on Media

Marshall McLuhan, the great Canadian media and culture theorist (1911–1980), explains his ideas about the social, cultural, and political impact of books in his book *Understanding Media: The Extensions of Man* (New York: McGraw-Hill). He writes (1965, pp. 172–173):

> Socially, the typographic extension of man brought in nationalism, industrialism, mass markets, and universal literacy and education. For print presented an image of repeatable precision that inspired totally new forms of extending social energies. Print released great psychic and social energies in the Renaissance, as today in Japan or Russia, by breaking the individual out of the traditional group while providing a model of how to add individual to individual in massive agglomeration of power. The same spirit of private enterprise that emboldened authors and artists to cultivate self-expression led other men to create giant corporations, both military and commercial.
>
> Perhaps the most significant of the gifts of typography to man is that of detachment and noninvolvement....The fragmenting and analytic power of the printed word in our psychic lives gave us that "dissociation of sensibility" which in the arts and literature since Cezanne and since Baudelaire has been a top priority for elimination in every program of reform in taste and knowledge.

Table 4.7 McLuhan on electronic and print media

Electronic media	Print media
The ear	The eye
All-at-once	Linearity
Simultaneity	Interconnectedness
Emotion	Logic
Radio	Books
Community	Individuality
Involvement	Detachment
Pattern recognition	Data classification

McLuhan argues that a change in the popularity of a medium has profound economic, political, social, and cultural consequences.

When we think about printed works on paper, for example, we must remember that they are objects and it is not only the ideas in books that are important but also the physical nature of books, the paper, and the printed matter in them which brings us ideas as well as stories, photos, pictures, and many other things.

It is the linearity of print and the fact that individuals who read printed matter can move through it at their own pace which fosters, McLuhan explains, rationality, individualism, and detachment. We can compare McLuhan's ideas about print media and electronic media in the chart below, which I made and is based on material found in *Understanding Media* (Table 4.7):

McLuhan wrote "The medium is the message" which argues that the impact of the media as media is more important than the texts they carry. Many people would not agree with this notion. McLuhan's ideas were out of favor for many years, in part because the jazzy style he used in writing alienated many academics. That has changed in recent years because of the utility of his ideas in dealing with the Internet and the digital world.

Another idea from McLuhan that is of interest to us in our investigation of the media involves his ideas about hot and cool media. As he explained in *Understanding Media* (1956, pp. 22–23):

> There is a basic principle that distinguishes a hot medium like radio from a cool one like the telephone, or a hot medium like the movie from a cool one like TV. A hot medium is one that extends one single sense in "high definition." High definition is the state of being well filled with data. A photograph is visually "high definition." A cartoon is "low definition," simply because very little visual information is provided. Telephone is a cool medium, or one of low definition, because the ear is given a meager amount of information. And speech is a cool medium of low definition, because so little is given and so much has to be filled in by the listener. On the other hand, hot media do not leave so much to be filled in or completed by the audience. Naturally, therefore, a hot medium like the radio has very different effects on the user from a cool medium like the telephone....

We can see the differences between the two kinds of media in the chart below. I have elicited the items in this chart from the material in the McLuhan

Table 4.8 McLuhan on hot and cool media

Hot media	Cool media
High definition	Low definition
Filled with data	Little data provided
Extends a single sense	No sense is dominant
Photograph	Cartoon
Radio	Telephone
First World Countries	Third World Countries
Films	Television
City slicker	Rustic
Past mechanical age	Present TV age
Lecture	Seminar
Videos	Twitter

selection and other sections of *Understanding Media* as well as from the implications of some of McLuhan's ideas (Table 4.8):

To this list, I have added videos and Twitter to bring McLuhan's analysis up to date. We have to recognize that hot and cool media have different social and political effects. A hot medium like radio provides a great deal more data or information than a cool one like the telephone or Twitter, and the effects of these different kinds of media are also different. Thus, a hot medium like radio is good for shaping the thinking of large groups of people, while a cool medium, like the telephone—or, in its newest incarnation, the mobile telephone, is not.

STATISTICS ON INTEREST IN THE MEDIA

I conclude this discussion of media and everyday life with statistics from Google on media and from Amazon.com books on books about the media (accessed 11/2/2021).

GOOGLING MEDIA

Media:	20,150,000,000 results
Media and Society	1,450,000,000 results
Media and Everyday Life	1,560,000,000 results

AMAZON BOOKS ON MEDIA

Media	70,000 books
Media and Society	60,000 books
Media and Everyday Life	10,000 books

Not only do we consume an enormous amount of media, but also we are interested in the role media play in our everyday lives and our societies.

REFERENCES

Berger, Arthur Asa. 1988. *Media USA*. 2nd ed. New York: Longman.
———. 2019. *Media analysis techniques*. 6th ed. Thousand Oaks, CA: Sage.
———. 2020. *Media and communication research methods*. 5th ed. Thousand Oaks, CA: Sage.
Denzin, Norman. 1991. *Images of postmodern society: Social theory and contemporary cinema*. London: Sage.
Douglas, Mary. 1977. In Defence of shopping. In *The shopping experience*, ed. P. Falk and C. Campbell, 15–30. London: Sage.
Dreyfus, Herbert L. 2009. *On the Internet*. 2nd ed. London: Routledge.
Haugen, Frances. 2021, October 6. Morning edition.
Illouz, Eva. 1998. The lost innocence of love: Romance as a postmodern condition. *Theory, Culture & Society* 15: 3–4.
Lakoff, George, and Mark Johnson. 1980. *Metaphors we live by*. Chicago, IL: University of Chicago Press.
Lotman, Yuri. 1977. *The structure of the artistic text*. Ann Arbor: Michigan Slavic Contributions.
Lyotard, Jean-François. 1984. *The postmodern condition: A report on knowledge*. Minneapolis: University of Minnesota Press.
McLuhan, Marshall. 1965. *Understanding media: The extensions of man*. New York: McGraw-Hill.
Radway, Janice. 1991. *Reading the romance: Women, patriarchy, and popular literature*. Chapel Hill: University of North Carolina Press.
Richardson, Laurel. 1990. Narrative and sociology. *Journal of Contemporary Ethnology* 19: 118.
Thompson, Michael, Richard Ellis, and Aaron Wildavsky. 1990. *Cultural theory*. Boulder, CO: Westview.
Wildavsky, Aaron. 1982. *Conditions for a pluralist democracy or cultural pluralism means more than one political culture in a country*. Unpublished manuscript.

CHAPTER 5

The Postmodern Sacred in America

Chapter Objectives The ideas of Emile Durkheim, a sociologist, and Mircea Eliade, a scholar of religion, are discussed as they relate to religion the sacred. Eliade is interested in the sacred and myth. This is followed by an analysis of the sacred and its relation to modernism and postmodernism which are compared again in a chart with some different topics than the first chart on the topic. The ideas of Jean-Francois Lyotard on postmodernism and the sacred are considered as well as the ideas of Jean Baudrillard on hyperreality and postmodernism and a comparison of the sacred and the profane. The chapter concludes with five case studies involving the sacred: football, presidential campaigns (with a focus on Donald Trump), marketing (with a comparison of department stores and cathedrals), pilgrims and tourists, and a postmodern novel, *The Crying of Lot 49*.

Keywords Sacred • Profane • Myth • Modernism • Postmodernism • Hyperreality

> **Sacred** describes something that is dedicated or set apart for the service or worship of a deity; is considered worthy of spiritual respect or devotion; or inspires awe or reverence among believers. The property is often ascribed to objects (a "sacred artifact" that is venerated and blessed), or places ("sacred ground").

> French sociologist Émile Durkheim considered the dichotomy between the sacred and the profane to be the central characteristic of religion: "religion is a unified system of beliefs and practices relative to *sacred things*, that is to say, things set apart and forbidden." In Durkheim's theory, the sacred represents the interests of the group, especially unity, which are embodied in sacred group symbols, or totems. The profane, on the other hand, involves mundane individual concerns.
>
> https://en.wikipedia.org/wiki/Sacred

> **Postmodernism** is an intellectual stance or mode of discourse[1][2] defined by an attitude of skepticism toward what it describes as the grand narratives and ideologies of modernism, as well as opposition to epistemic certainty and the stability of meaning.[3] It questions or criticizes viewpoints associated with Enlightenment rationality dating back to the 17th century,[4] and is characterized by irony, eclecticism, and its rejection of the "universal validity" of binary oppositions, stable identity, hierarchy, and categorization. Postmodernism is associated with relativism and a focus on ideology in the maintenance of economic and political power.[4] Postmodernists are generally "skeptical of explanations which claim to be valid for all groups, cultures, traditions, or races," and describe truth as relative.[7] It can be described as a reaction against attempts to explain reality in an objective manner by claiming that reality is a mental construct.[7] Access to an unmediated reality or to objectively rational knowledge is rejected on the grounds that all interpretations are contingent on the perspective from which they are made;[8] as such, claims to objective fact are dismissed as naive realism.[4]
>
> https://en.wikipedia.org/wiki/Postmodernism

I will begin by discussing the notion of the sacred and then I will deal with my analysis of selected elements of the postmodern sacred in America.

On the Sacred
In Emile Durkheim's classic book, *The Elementary Forms of the Religious Life*, first published in 1912, he distinguishes between the sacred and the profane. He writes (1965, pp. 52, 53):

All known religious beliefs, whether simple or complex, present one common characteristic: they presuppose a classification of all things, real and ideal, of which men think, into two classes or opposed groups, generally designated by the worlds *profane* and *sacred*....This division of the world into two domains, the containing all that is sacred, the other all that is profane, is the distinctive trait of religious thought: the beliefs, myths, dogmas, and legends are either representations or systems of representations which express the nature of sacred things, the virtues and powers that are attributed to them, or their relations with each other and with profane things....In all the history of human thought there e exists no other example of two categories of things so profoundly differentiated or so radically opposed to one another.

Durkheim's analysis of the difference between the sacred and the profane suggests that it is the most important opposition in human thought and that the two realms, the sacred and the profane, are mutually exclusive.

His analysis sets the stage for a more contemporary study of these two domains by Mircea Eliade, who was chairman of the Department of the History of Religion at the University of Chicago and the author of many books on religion (Fig. 5.1).

Eliade is interested in "sacredness," and the relation of myth to history and time. His conceptions have relevance to my idea of myth as a model and the matter previously mentioned: that man put himself in the center of the universe in the Alger myth. What Eliade says is that man puts himself in the center of the universe in all myths.

Fig. 5.1 Mircea Eliade

The following analysis is based upon one of Eliade's best-known books, *The Sacred and The Profane*, which deals with religious myth, symbolism, and ritual. Eliade is a rather controversial figure (both for his methodology and his political allegiances), but I find that his ideas are very useful in interpreting American culture as well as myth.

Eliade, like Durkheim before him, makes a basic distinction between two realms: the sacred and the profane, which he says are "two modes of being." The sacred involves such things as religious feelings, the irrational, and the unnatural. The sacred is "numinous," which means revealing "divine power" and of a different order from the profane and natural order of the world. Sacredness has a certain existential quality and, through it, man participates in "reality" in a certain way--and it also informs our ideas about time and space. For Eliade, there is what he describes as sacred time and sacred space which are qualitatively different from profane time and space. I will say more about these topics shortly (Fig. 5.2).

What concerns Eliade is the relation that exists between the sacred and myth. He explains (1961, p. 95):

> The myth relates a sacred history, that is, a primordial event that took place at the beginning of time, ab Initio. But to relate a sacred history is equivalent to revealing a mystery. For the persons of the myth are not human beings; they are gods or culture heroes and ~ -or this reason, their qesta constitute mysteries; man could not know their acts if' they were not revealed to him. The myth, then, is the history of what took place in illo tempore, the recital of what the gods or the semi-divine beings did at the beginning of time. To tell a myth is to proclaim what happened ab origine. Once told, that is, revealed, the myth becomes apodictic truth; it establishes a truth that is absolute

Fig. 5.2 Theseus Killing the Minotaur

The function of myth, as Eliade sees it, is to give an explanation of the beginning of things and provide a model for future action. This model has the advantage of supplying apodictic or "certain" knowledge. As Eliade puts it (1961, pp. 96, 97):

> This is the aspect of myth that demands particular emphasis here. The myth reveals absolute sacrality, because it relates the creative activity of the gods, unveils the sacredness of their work. In other words, the myth describes the various and sometimes dramatic irruptions of the sacred into the world.

I might add that by sacred, Eliade doesn't mean pious religiosity associated with institutional religion. This myth becomes "the paradigmatic model for all human activities."

For Eliade, the outstanding characteristic of modern life is the "desacralization of human existence" and the existence and the creation of profane man. But profane man is built upon the rejection or sacred man, which means that the sacred still has a large role in man's consciousness and unconscious.

The vestiges of sacred man still remain to "haunt" modern man, despite all that he does, for man cannot escape from his past or from history. What remains, says Eliade, are "camouflaged myths and degenerated rituals," such as New Year parties, wedding celebrations, and so forth. He mentions the mythical motifs used in the cinema and literature (1961, p. 205):

> A whole volume could well be written on the myths of modern man, on the mythologies camouflaged in the plays that he enjoys, in the books that he reads. The cinema, that "dream factory," takes over and employs countless mythical motifs—the fight between hero and monster, initiatory combats and ordeals, paradigmatic figures and images (the maiden, the hero, the paradisal landscape, hell, and so on).

Since one of the functions of myth is to remove us from profane time and place us in sacred time, when we are at the beginning of things and time does not exist, even reading books is "mythological," since it allows us to "kill time." What all of this means, then, is that modern man isn't as irreligious as he thinks, for according to Eliade (1961, pp. 205–206):

> The great majority of the irreligious are not liberated from religious behavior, from theologies and mythologies. They sometimes stagger under a whole magico-religious paraphernalia, which, however, has degenerated to the point of caricature and hence is hard to recognize for what it is.

In this respect, he mentions little religions, social utopias, Marxism (based on one of the great eschatological myths, that of "the redeeming role of the just") sexual freedom movements, and nudism. He also sees the initiatory aspects of the sacred appearing, though modified, in psychoanalysis.

I dealt with postmodernism, in general terms, earlier in the book. In the material that follows, there is a certain amount of duplication that I could not avoid since I wish to treat the topic in more detail now.

Postmodernism generally is understood to have come about by an almost instantaneous change in many societies. It is similar to one to modernism described by Virginia Woolf many years ago. She writes:

> On or about December 1910, human character changed. I am not saying that one went out, as one might into a garden, and there saw a rose had flowered, or that a hen had laid an egg. The change was not like that. But a change there was, nevertheless, and since one must be arbitrary, let us date it about the year 1910.... When human relations change, there is at the same time a change in religion, conduct, politics, and literature.

Woolf gave her lecture in 1924 "Mr. Bennett and Mrs. Brown" at a meeting of the Heretics Club at Cambridge University. She argued that after December 1910 (or around then) life in England had changed in major ways—a change that she noticed in the relationships between husbands and wives, masters and servants, children and parents, and the kind of literature that was being written.

Modernism and Postmodernism
Scholars have described this change as the advent of modernism, which is reflected in the work of writers such as Ezra Pound, James Joyce, and Robert Musil and philosophers and thinkers such as Freud, Marx, Nietzsche, and Darwin. Modernism also had a profound impact on everyday life, as Wolf noted.

Woolf was born in 1892 and died in 1941. That means she was 18 in the month when, as she explained things, the world changed and her life and her writings were, we must assume, profoundly affected by the changes she described. It is reasonable to suggest that not long after Woolf died, the period known as postmodernism began.

Postmodernism is, whatever else it might be, a term involving periodization: it comes after modernism. Scholars of postmodernism suggest that somewhere between the end of the Second World War and 1960, the world changed again—there was a global mutation and the era of postmodernism dawned.

And, like the modernism that it replaced, postmodernism profoundly affected everyday life, relations between people, as well as literature and the arts. Let me suggest it was on or about in December of 1960, which will give modernism a 50-year reign.

Modernism and postmodernism differ in many ways. I deal with some of them in the chart below. To offer a set of paired opposites, I've had to simplify certain things and my chart is somewhat reductionist, but it does offer us a way of seeing some of the basic components of modernism and postmodernism. I should add that some (maybe many) scholars now consider postmodernism to be passé and suggest that we are now in a post-postmodern period which, so far, has resisted our ability to find a name for it.

Post-postmodernism we may regard as an example of hyper-periodization, though some scholars suggest that postmodernism is only a different form of modernism and is in actuality only a name for an advanced form of capitalism.

I've used paired opposites because, according to Ferdinand de Saussure, that's the way we make sense of concepts. As he explained (and I quoted him earlier on this matter) in his *Course in General Linguistics* (1966, p. 117) "concepts are purely differential and defined not by their positive content but negatively by their relations with the other terms of the system" and "the most precise characteristic" of concepts "is in being what the others are not."

I offer here a variation of the chart on modernism and postmodernism that I provided earlier in the book. It has some additional topics related to modernism and postmodernism that are worth considering (Table 5.1).

This chart provides a good overview of some of the main differences between the two periods. The "post" in postmodernism means "coming after" but it can also mean "moving beyond" or "the opposite of." If you investigate "modernism" and "postmodernism" using Google search you find the following results (as of 8/22/2021) (Table 5.2):

The postmodern and the sacred seem, at first sight, to be opposites. After all, Jean-François Lyotard explained to us, in his book *The Postmodern Condition: A Report on Knowledge,* that postmodernism can be defined as involving "incredulity toward metanarratives." Metanarratives are the all-embracing philosophical systems such as those found in religion and philosophy that characterized modernist thinking.

Table 5.1 Modernism and postmodernism compared

Modernism	*Postmodernism*
After Dec. 10, 1910	After 1960 (more or less)
Metanarratives	Incredulity toward metanarratives
Unified, coherent self	Fragmented, decentered self
Seriousness	Playfulness
Robert Musil	Thomas Pynchon
Pablo Picasso	Andy Warhol
Sexual boundaries strong	Sexual boundaries weak
Family unit strong	Family unit weak
Marriage	The "affair," hooking up"
Print culture	Electronic culture
Encyclopedia Britannica	Wikipedia
Books	Cell phones, tablets
New York architecture	Las Vegas architecture
Mies Van der Rohe	Philip Johnson (AT&T skyscraper)
Unitary works of art	The pastiche
High culture/pop culture difference	De-differentiation: high culture/pop
Production society (make)	Consumer cultures (buy)
Reality	Hyperreality
America	Disneyland

Table 5.2 Results on Google for modernism and postmodernism searches

Topic	Number of results
Modernism	92,900,000
Postmodernism	38,900,000
Postmodernism definition	36,900,000

He writes (1984, pp. xxiii, xxiv):

> The object of this study is the condition of knowledge in most highly developed societies. I have decided to use the word *postmodern* to describe that condition. The word is in current use on the American continent among sociologists and critics; it designates the state of our culture following the transformations which, since the end of the nineteenth century, have altered the game rules for science, literature, and the arts. The present study will place these transformations in the context of the crisis of narratives....Simplifying to the extreme, I define *postmodern* as incredulity toward metanarratives. To the obsolescence of the metanarrative apparatus of legitimation corresponds, most notably, the crisis of metaphysical philosophy and of the university institution which in the past relied on it.

Lyotard asserts that in postmodern societies there are competing narratives and many different ways of making sense of the world, which has led to what he describes as a crisis of legitimation. We don't know what's right and what's wrong. In addition to our not knowing what to believe, many postmodern theorists argue that it doesn't make any difference what we believe.

There are many differences between postmodernism and modernism. If modernism differentiates between elite arts, such as opera and ballet, and popular culture, postmodernism tears down the barriers between them and revels joyfully in mass culture.

Postmodern texts have quick cuts and unexpected changes in them, have dissociated personalities, and generally lack a coherent narrative line. Modernism involves a stance of "high seriousness" toward life, whereas postmodernism involves an element of game playing and an ironic stance as well as a kind of playfulness (Fig. 5.3).

People in postmodernist societies "play" with their identities and change them when they feel bored with their old ones. And postmodern societies, as Jean Baudrillard suggests, are characterized by illusions and simulations. Reality, he suggests, has been replaced by *hyperreality*, a situation in which the sign is now more important than the signifier it stands for. As Peter Brooker explains in *Cultural Theory: A Glossary* (1999, pp. 121–122):

> Hyperreality. A term associated with the effects of MASS PRODUCTION and REPRODUCTION and suggesting that an object, event, experience so reproduced replaces or is preferred to its original: that the copy is "more real than real." In the writings of the French social philosopher and commentator on POSTMODERNISM, Jean Baudrillard (1929–), and Umberto Eco (1932–), hyperreality is associated especially with cultural tendencies and a prevailing sensibility in contemporary American society. In Baudrillard's discussion, hyperreality is synonymous with the most developed form of SIMULATION: the autonomous simulacra which is free from all reference to the real.

Fig. 5.3 Jean Baudrillard

That explains why Baudrillard believes that simulations are now more important and more real for people than the reality they were designed to imitate. Indeed, Baudrillard has even suggested that Disneyland is now the ultimate reality and the USA is an imitation of it! As the power of the Disney media corporation grows—and it has recently purchased Marvel comics and its heroes and Star Wars and its heroes—some theorists argue that it is now playing a dominating role in shaping our collective consciousness.

Postmodernism and the Sacred
Earlier I discussed Eliade's notion that many contemporary activities of men and women, which seem profane, are camouflaged versions of sacred ones. In a different book of his, *The Myth of the Eternal Return,* he offers some insights that help explain the sacred aspects of phenomena that might seem to be profane. As he explains (Pantheon books, 1954, pp. 27–28):

> We might say that the archaic world knows nothing of "profane" activities; every act which has a definite meaning—hunting, fishing, agriculture, games, conflicts, sexuality—in some way participates in the sacred....The only profane activities are those which have no mythical meaning, that is, which lack exemplary models. Thus, we may say that every responsible activity in pursuit of a definite end is, for the archaic world, a ritual.

What we arrive at is a world of polar opposites between the sacred and the profane. I spell these out in the chart I made that follows (Table 5.3):

These oppositions are in some cases extreme, but they serve to point out the difference between the sacred and the profane. From the sacred perspective, settling a country "consecrates" it and privileges it, making it the "center of the world."

Table 5.3 The sacred and the profane

The Sacred	The Profane
Consecrates a territory	Moves somewhere
It becomes the center of the world	Space is homogenous, undifferentiated
Lives in sacred space	No significance to the location
Experiences the "numinous"	All experiences the same
Symbols reveal the sacred	Symbols all are profane
Time is circular, recoverable	Time is linear
The world is renewed annually	World just exists
Myths (sacred histories) retold continually	Myths are seen as stories about gods
Heroes are paradigmatic models	Heroes are individuals, achievers
Nature full of religious symbols	Nature a retreat from civilization
Agriculture is a sacred calling	Agriculture is a job
Autochthony (importance of place)	Culture

The sacred perspective suggests that symbols are full of meaning and reveal the sacred, speaking to the whole man and woman. Nature is full of religious symbols which helps explain why many people experience profound emotions when immersed in certain natural settings.

Time is cyclical—recoverable, regainable, and repeatable—through the repetition of the proper rituals. Our myths, which are sacred histories, are reflected in our culture heroes and heroines, paradigmatic figures who serve as models for us to emulate and who reflect important values and beliefs. From the sacred perspective, man and woman are *autochthonous,* which means there is a profound connection between a country and the people who inhabit it.

Contemporary men and women may try to convince themselves that they are completely secular, but underneath the appearances, if Eliade is correct, we have the sacred flourishing and informing our behavior. Everything he cites, from reading novels to celebrating New Year's Eve with parties (and sometimes orgies), are examples of camouflaged sacred rituals.

We can apply Eliade's views to American culture and society. My argument has been that the American experience mirrors to a remarkable degree the various elements of the sacred experiences as delineated by Eliade. We were blessed with "nature" (the Frontier) and settled a great territory. We "sacralized" America in doing so. We occupied the true "center" of the earth (and we believe we still do) and escaped from history and profane time in founding our nation and we generated mythic heroes who showed us how to live sacred lives.

Now that we have a better understanding of the nature of postmodernism and of the sacred, and how it relates to the profane, I will discuss some elements of contemporary American life that have, I believe, a sacred dimension to them. People who are involved in these camouflaged sacred activities do not recognize that they are sacred, but the powerful emotions these activities generate in people give us good reason to suspect that more is going on in them than meets the eye.

Fig. 5.4 Football stadium

So, not only are many modern activities camouflaged versions of ancient sacred ones, if we can find a sacred or ritualistic dimension to an activity, we can see that it is sacred in its origins and nature, even if people involved in an activity don't recognize that to be the case (Fig. 5.4).

CASE STUDY 1: FOOTBALL AS A SACRED RITUAL

Let me begin by saying something about the sacred origin of sports contests. The first Olympics were held in 776 BC and, according to some scholars, were established by Hercules, after he had finished with his labors, to honor his father Zeus. The Olympics, which featured many different sports contests, were to be held every 4 years.

The official Olympics website says the Olympics started in 684 BC and included running, the long jump, javelin throwing, wrestling, boxing, discus throwing, and the shot put. Over the years, the Olympics evolved; until now there are summer and winter Olympics and they include many other sports.

There are, then, sacred roots to all athletic contests, but not all of them are as complex as a football match. If you change the discus to a football and include running and modified wrestling (the line play), you get the game of football. On many Saturdays, I watch college football games. These games are remarkable spectacles. I'm always amazed by the size of the stadiums in which these games are played. They take place in gigantic stadiums that hold seventy or eighty or even one hundred thousand spectators, many of whom are students and fans of the universities that are playing each other.

These stadiums are sacred spaces in universities. Entering a stadium releases one from the profane world and establishes one in a sacred world where sacred rituals are performed. One also moves beyond ordinary time because, in football, time is sacred. Every second in a game counts. The development of "instant replay" means that time repeats itself, what Eliade described as circular, and is not lost. When you watch a game on television, sometimes you see

Fig. 5.5 Football game. Photo by the Author from Television

the same play several times, from different perspectives, when officials decide to review a play.

Viewers of televised football games see a different game than people who are at the stadium, due to the power of television to provide different shots of plays and players and make the games more dramatic. Also, you have the commentators offering their insights into the events in the game. Now, with the advent of gigantic screens in many stadiums, people attending a game can also see how it is being televised and thus have the best of both worlds, so to speak.

Visually the games are exciting. You have the huge stadiums full of people wearing the colors of their teams, you have the lush green of the football field, you have the uniforms of the players and the officials, you have the uniformed marching band players, and you often have a beautiful blue sky. Visually speaking, a football game is very stimulating (Fig. 5.5).

The spectators/fans often wear the colors of their team, paint their faces with their school's colors, and become very emotional. It is not unusual for some fans of a losing team to cry, especially after a game in which the school these fans are attending loses in the last minute of a game—sometimes in the last seconds of a game. Then, there is often a gigantic groan, as fifty thousand fans of a losing team, in unison, express their dismay. The fans of the winning team, on the other hand, are ecstatic.

You only get these extreme emotions in very close games that are decided during the last minutes or seconds of a game. The fans of teams that are losing by large margins and have no chance of winning sit there, sadly, with stoic resignation, while those fans supporting the winning teams feel very happy.

The teams playing one another usually have marching bands with eighty or a hundred musicians in them, all in costume, who play at certain times on the sidelines, such as when a touchdown is scored, and then perform intricate formations during the break between the halves of the game. And some cheerleaders perform on the sidelines. They lead their team's fans in cheers and dance, tumble, and try to entertain people at the game. The women cheerleaders often are scantily dressed and wiggle their bodies in some dances. There is, then, a sexual element to cheerleading and some would say to other aspects of the game as well.

There are often symbolic figures or animals who represent the team, such as the person who rides a white horse and is all dressed up like a knight when the University of Southern California "Trojans" play other teams. The Arkansas "Razorbacks" have a huge hog with them at their games. These animals are totem figures who, it is hoped, will bring blessings to their teams.

The football players wear colorful uniforms with their numbers and their names. They wear helmets and teeth braces to protect them and shoulder pads that enhance their masculinity. In recent years, since we've discovered that many professional football players suffered concussions and serious brain damage, young children are not showing as much interest in playing the games that they used to show. Doctors started noticing how many concussions players experienced and how impaired many--perhaps most--professional football players were, from accidents of one kind or another during the games.

Many parents won't let their children play football in high schools. The players are seen as heroes and can be seen as modern manifestations of ancient mythological heroes whose remarkable achievements made them famous.

In my book *Media Analysis Techniques*, 6th edition (2019), I discuss professional football as a functional alternative to religion, but we can say the same thing about college football.

The chart below is based on the one in my book that compares football to religion and suggests that football is a functional alternative to religion in many ways, suggesting, for example, that superstars are analogous to saints and the complex plays in football are similar to theology (Table 5.4).

Michael Real, an astute critic of popular culture, has written about the Super Bowl as a mythic spectacle, but what he says about the Super Bowl can apply

Table 5.4 Football as a functional alternative to religion

Football	Religion
Superstars	Saints
Saturday game	Service
Ticket	Offering
Complex plays	Theology
Players on way to the championship game	Knights in search of the Holy Grail
Coaches	Clergy
Stadiums	Churches
Fans	Congregations
Instant replay	Time is circular

to collegiate football as well. He writes that in secular societies, sports "fill the vacuum" left by America's (and other countries) noninvolvement with organized religion. We can see, from the chart, that football has many parallels with religion, enough so that we can say football is a sacred activity and a kind of religion for many people.

David Biderman, in the January 15, 2010, issue of the *Wall Street Journal*, offers some statistics about a typical three-hour television game broadcast:

11 minutes of actual playing time.
17 minutes of replays
4 seconds is the length of actual play
67 minutes involved with huddles, etc.
75 minutes for commercials
3 seconds devoted to cheerleaders
40 seconds allowed for the offensive team to snap the ball

If a typical play lasts 4 s, there could—in theory—be 15 plays in a minute, if the teams didn't have huddles or use their time in other ways. If a team takes 40 s to snap the ball and a play takes 4 s, you get approximately one play a minute.

The reasons people become passionate about football involve their identification with the colleges playing the game, the fact that many rivalries go back for 80 or 90 years (or more), and the dramatic nature of football. There are also occasionally upsets in which lower-ranked teams defeat higher-ranked teams.

Sports contests, we must recognize, are dramas and generate powerful catharses, as I mentioned above in my discussion of the 50,000-person or 100,000-person collective "groan" at the end of close games. I would describe a game as being like an iceberg. The game is the tip of the iceberg rising above the water, but most of the iceberg, the unconscious, lies below the water and is not recognized by us, but this unconscious plays a major role in our behavior and the emotions that are stirred both in religious ceremonies and in football games. My argument is that football games can be seen as sacred and thus, though we are not aware that this is the case, have elements of religious ceremonies about them.

Postmodernism is based on de-differentiation, minimizing the differences between elite culture and popular culture and between many other domains. Seeing football as a sacred activity similar in nature to attending church is, then, a very postmodern approach. Baseball, on the other hand, is a modernist game. It is a nineteenth-century pastoral game that is not concerned about time. Games can last, in some cases, 3 or 4 h or longer. But baseball also can generate incredible tension at times and very powerful cathartic responses (Fig. 5.6).

Fig. 5.6 Washington monument

CASE STUDY 2: RUNNING FOR PRESIDENT

In Great Britain, the campaign for the Prime Minister's position lasts 2 months. In the USA, the campaign for the presidency lasts 2 years, but much longer than that since politicians and others who wish to run for the presidency start planning their campaigns the day after a president is inaugurated. Eighteen months before the election for president, in November of 2016, there were more than a dozen Republican candidates and five Democratic candidates for the presidency, and there were televised debates that attracted the attention of millions of Americans. The candidates also spent a great deal of time at rallies and other political events.

The candidates also devoted a great deal of time and effort getting money for their campaigns because it costs many hundreds of millions of dollars to run for president. The money is needed for the campaign and organizing staffs and advertising—mostly on television and the Internet.

An article recently was published that claimed 158 families supplied most of the money fueling the campaigns of the candidates in both parties. This means that millionaires and billionaires play an important role in American politics. A report in the *New York Times* Internet site by Nicholas Confessore, Sarah Cohen, and Karen Yourish explains:

> The 158 families each contributed $250,000 or more in the campaign through June 30, according to the most recent available Federal Election Commission filings and other data, while an additional 200 families gave more than $100,000. Together, the two groups contributed well over half the money in the presidential election -- the vast majority of it supporting Republicans.
> https://www.nytimes.com/interactive/2015/10/11/us/...

The families that are supporting these candidates are doing so for ideological reasons and because they believe that a Republican president will be more amenable to taxation and other policies benefitting these families and the corporations they own and run.

It is fair to suggest that running for president is an ordeal and the candidates have taken on the character of mythical heroes in the public imagination.

Several of the candidates on the Republic side were wealthy and were brought up in privileged families. Consider the 2016 campaign for the presidency. One candidate, Jeb Bush, is the son of a former president and brother of a former president. He raised more than 100 million dollars for his campaign. The Bush family is very wealthy.

Another Republican candidate, Carly Fiorina, is worth $80 million and Donald Trump is worth an estimated 4 billion dollars, but many people consider that figure to be highly inflated. But Senator Marco Rubio, from Florida, is, supposedly, worth only $450,000 and one of his claims to fame is that he comes from a poor family (Fig. 5.7).

A number of the candidates for the Republican nomination made the same claim—to show that they are "ordinary" people and that American culture's open quality and social mobility have made it possible for them to achieve whatever eminence they have.

America is a place, as Rubio puts it, "where anyone from anywhere can be anything." Ben Carson, a distinguished neurosurgeon, continually pointed out that he grew up in a poor family and that his life chances looked bleak, but he was able to overcome adversity and become a surgeon.

The theme of overcoming adversity and rising to great heights is a common theme found in mythological heroes. In Carl G. Jung's *Man and His Symbols*, Joseph L. Henderson has a chapter on "Ancient Myths and Modern Man" which deals with the myth of the hero. The 2016 Republican presidential candidates had some elements of this myth in their life stories. The mythic hero, Henderson explains (1968, p. 101):

Fig. 5.7 Trump rally. Photo by the Author from Television Coverage

These hero myths vary enormously in detail, but the more closely we examine them the more one sees that they are structurally similar....Over and over again one hears a tale describing the hero's miraculous but humble birth, his early proof of superhuman strength, his rapid rise to prominence or power, his triumphant struggle with the forces of evil, his fallibility to the sin of pride (*hybris*) and his fall through betrayal or a "heroic" sacrifice that ends in his death.

We have to make certain modifications in this myth and substitute political success for superhuman strength and see the Democratic Party for the forces of evil. The sacrifice a Presidential candidate makes is to "temporarily suspend his or her campaign" when there is no hope of success. The matter of a humble birth extends to Democrats as well. Barack Obama's parents were not wealthy and he had the added disadvantage of being black.

Donald Trump cannot claim to have been born poor but he does latch on to the "superhuman strength" aspect of the myth when he talks about his prowess as a businessman and the fact that he is very rich. Some would say he also has a considerable amount of "hubris," which we can define as an extreme amount of pride, self-confidence, and self-admiration, reaching the level of narcissism. Some psychoanalysts have described him as a "malignant narcissist," based on his behavior for many years, and especially while president.

My point is that there is a mythic aspect to the campaigns of the candidates for the presidency in both parties. There are also certain rituals that candidates for the presidency must observe such as meeting people from Iowa and New Hampshire in small restaurants and talking with them "face-to-face;" attending fundraising events at the homes of wealthy supporters to get money for the campaign; speaking at rallies where supporters come to see the candidates they favor; and nowadays, having a presence in social media.

Donald Trump used Twitter a great deal (until he was barred from using it in January 2021) to attack other candidates and the Democratic candidates. A sample of one of his self-congratulatory tweets I found on October 12th follows:

> Great, everyone is saying I did much better on @60Minutes last week than President Obama did tonight. I agree!
> More
> President Obama was terrible on @60Minutes tonight. He said CLIMATE CHANGE is the most important thing, not all of the current disasters!
> Donald J. Trump @realDonaldTrump

I discuss Trump in some detail in my book *Three Tropes on Trump*, published by Peter Lang in 2020.

In all the presidential elections, wealthy supporters of candidates, both Democratic and Republican, spend hundreds of millions of dollars and more backing the choice of each party. The 2012 election for president cost more than 2 billion dollars and the 2016 election topped that at 6.5 billion dollars. The 2020 election is estimated to have cost 11 billion dollars.

Fig. 5.8 Consume

Trump is the first billionaire to run for the presidency which suggests that wealthy people in America—at least some of them—now have decided to become president rather than merely supporting a candidate for the presidency who will serve their policies. All presidential candidates hope to spend at least four and probably eight years in the center of American political sacred space, the White House, which is also, politically speaking, as some American politicians see it, the center of the political world. Trump was defeated in the 2020 presidential election which he lost by more than seven million votes, becoming what for him was the worst possible thing—a big loser (Fig. 5.8).

CASE STUDY 3: SELLING AND THE SACRED

John Calvin told us to live well, but not in excess, which means being a consumer but not letting consumption completely dominate one's life, and I've mentioned Max Weber's work on the Protestant ethic. Now I would live to deal with the sacred roots of consumption and the psychological imperatives that drive us toward consumption.

Eliade privileges the home as the primary locus of consumption. It is a sacred space in which we live and into which we bring the many things we buy that we need to live: food, furniture, clothing, and everything else we need, and in many cases, don't need but want. Our homes are, existentially speaking, our centers of the world (Fig. 5.9).

According to the social anthropologist Mary Douglas, whose ideas I discussed earlier in the book, our decisions about what to buy are generally based on unconscious imperatives that come from the lifestyles with which we

Fig. 5.9 John Calvin

identify. She cautioned us to remember that the choices we make when shopping are not based on individual psychology but, instead, on rejecting the kinds and brands of things members of other lifestyles like.

Ernest Dichter, a marketing expert and the father of motivational research, made a general point that is relevant here. He wrote, in *The Strategy of Desire* (Dichter 1960, p. 12):

> Whatever your attitude toward modern psychology or psychoanalysis, it has been proved beyond any doubt that many of our daily decisions are governed by motivations over which we have no control and of which we are quite unaware. These motivations are lodged deep in our unconscious and are based, to a considerable degree, on the sacred nature of the act of consumption.

An article titled "The Sacred and the Profane in Consumer Behavior: Theodicy and The Odyssey" by Russell W. Belk, Melanie Wallendorf, and John F. Sherry, Jr., that appeared in *The Journal of Consumer Behavior* (Vol. 16, No. 1, June 1989, pp. 1–38) deals in considerable detail with the sacred nature of consumption, using ideas from Eliade and many other scholars. The authors write (1989, p. 10):

> Consumption also has its public cathedrals that enhance the mystery and sense of otherworldliness of the sacred. Such places have been instrumental in the development of consumer cultures. Perhaps the most influential of these has been the department store. Rather than following the wheel of the retailing pattern of

entering the market as low-price institutions, turn-of-the-century department stores entered the market as extravagant show places where functional and financial considerations paled in the magnificence of their grandiose architecture, theatrical lighting, and sumptuous display....Today, the simple department store is eclipsed in grandeur by the shopping mall....where shopping has become a ritual in a consumption-oriented society.

The authors consider any number of aspects of the sacred in their article, including discussions of the "sacralization of the secular" in music and popular culture, and the nature of sacred space and time, among other things. They also discuss several aspects of the sacred, such as the importance of myth, mystery, ritual, hierophany (the manifestation of the sacred), and ecstasy.

Many of these concepts are drawn from Eliade, Durkheim, and other scholars. Many objects obtain a sacred dimension by becoming part of a ritual that transforms them, by being connected to a pilgrimage to stores with special qualities, and that kind of thing.

A German media scholar, Wolfgang Haug, discusses changes in the role of department stores in language that has religious overtones. He discusses a text *The Key To The Consumer* in his book *Critique of Commodity Aesthetics: Appearance, Sexuality, and Advertising in Capitalist Society* and writes (1986, pp. 68–69):

Commodities are no longer to be displayed in their traditional categories "but should be arranged thematically to fulfill the needs and desires of the buyers." One must not confront the buyer brusquely with a commodity but "guide them into the 'entertainment.'" So it can be seen that even the miracle of the transubstantiation of value from the commodity's use-form into the value-form of money, under the pressure of capital's anxieties, can be turned into a mysterious cult, an initiation ceremony for the buyer lured into acting as the saviour of exchange-value....The exhibition of commodities, their inspection, the act of purchase, and all the associated moments, are integrated into the concept of one theatrical total work of art which plays upon the public's willingness to buy. Thus, the saleroom is designed as a stage, purpose-built to convey entertainment to its audience that will stimulate a heightened desire to buy. "On this stage the sale is initiated. This stage is the most important element in sales promotion."

Haug quotes Kauffman (no first name given), the author of *The Key to the Consumer*, as follows (1986, p. 69):

The entertainment stage at the Globus department store became a mecca to which retailers from all over the world made an annual pilgrimage.

There, Haug adds, "they hoped to gain access to the Holy of Holies," and learn more about how to design successful department stores. What we are dealing with is what Haug calls the "aestheticization" of department stores and the stylization of the selling process.

Some years ago I became interested in department stores and their relationship to the sacred. I happened to be on a radio talk show with Stanley Marcus and when I told him I thought there was a relationship between department stores and cathedrals he said "Of course. In ancient times you found all kinds of things being sold on the grounds of cathedrals. So there's an obvious connection between the two."

In many countries, you still find objects—generally of a religious nature—being sold on the grounds of cathedrals or in streets and squares near them. What follows shortly is a chart that suggests that department stores can be seen as functional alternatives to cathedrals. Many of the things we associate with cathedrals exist, in a secularized form, in department stores (Fig. 5.10).

I should point out that now, with the development of the Internet, a great deal of consumer behavior has switched to sites such as Amazon.com. Department stores are fighting back with their own Internet sites, a phenomenon known as "bricks and clicks." Many department stores have gone out of business but some, such as Macy's, still are hanging on, though in greatly diminished form since the eruption of the coronavirus in March 2020. In the chart below, I suggest that department stores can be seen as functional alternatives to cathedrals (Table 5.5).

This chart shows that in many different ways, what we experience in department stores is similar in nature, though desacralized, to what we experience in cathedrals. Both, I suggest, can be seen as sacred spaces where people have powerful emotional experiences.

In *The Waning of the Middle Ages*, historian Johan Huizinga describes how the two realms—the sacred and the secular—merge into one another. He writes (1924, p. 156):

Fig. 5.10 Cathedral in Barcelona

Table 5.5 Department store as functional alternative to cathedral

Department store	Cathedral
Modern	Medieval
Paradisiacal: Heaven on Earth Now	Paradisiacal: Heaven in the Future
Passion: Merchandising	Passion: Salvation
Sales: Save Money	Prayer: Save Souls
Sacred Texts: Catalogs, brochures	Sacred Texts: Bible, Prayer Books
Clerks	Clergy
Sell: Products	Sell: God
Possessions Signs of Spiritual Election	Holiness Sign of Spiritual Election
Big Sales Days	Religious Holidays
Sale of an Expensive Product	Conversion of a Sinner
Buy Incredible Gifts	Experience Miracles
Pay Taxes	Pay Tithe
Muzac	Religious Music
Lighting to Sell	Lighting to Inspire Reverence
Bad Credit	Penance
Advertising	Proselytizing
Cash Register	Offering Plate
Brand Loyalty	Devotion

> All life was saturated with religion to such an extent that the people were in constant danger of losing sight of the distinction between things spiritual and things temporal. If, on the one hand, all the details of ordinary life may be raised to a sacred level, on the other hand, all that is holy sinks to the commonplace, by the fact of being blended with everyday life.

In contemporary consumer cultures our lives are saturated with commercials and other forms of advertising: on the radio, on our smartphones, on any screen one might imagine. Beneath these advertisements and fueling our desire to consume more and more products is, I would suggest, an unconscious feeling or sense that our actions have an ultimately religious or sacred dimension to them; they are a means of showing our "election" (a good Puritan term) and that we are the worthy benefactors of God's grace (Fig. 5.11).

One last consideration. We can apply Jonathan Edwards' ideas about freedom and determination to consumer behavior. Edwards was trying to reconcile man's "freedom" and an all-powerful God. Edwards explained that we can act as we please but we cannot please as we please. If we substitute "buy" for "act" we find that we can buy as we please but not please as we please.

We might be able to buy anything we want, but God (or some entity acting in his name (such as advertising agencies) influences or determines what we want. Some higher force is determining what pleases us and, in the context of this discussion, it would be some manifestation of the sacred. Thus, brand advocates can be seen as secularized versions of religious proselytizers, and purchasing a different brand of a product or service is a kind of religious conversion (Fig. 5.12).

Fig. 5.11 Jonathan Edwards

Fig. 5.12 Travel photos of Arthur Asa Berger

Case Study 4: Pilgrims and Cruise Passengers

Over the millennia, pilgrims have traveled to sacred spaces to pray, worship their divinities, and perform certain rites. So the notion that travel can have a sacred dimension is not difficult to sustain. Consider the passion in a commentary by Samuel Jemsel about the nature of his travels (quoted in Adler, *Jewish Travelers*, and 1930, p. 329):

> I was possessed by a violent and insatiable desire to visit the places of God...as I had learnt that eminent men such as Rabbi Isaac and Rabbi Solomon Levi had also been inflamed with the desire of accomplishing the holy journey. I, being urged on like them by a sort of divine instinct, did not lose sight of the execution of my project: I would not have suffered myself to be turned aside from it by any

reason whatsoever. The desire to set out which had formed itself in my mind was so violent that it was impossible for me to remain in my own home, or to go about my accustomed business.

Jemsel's religious passion overwhelmed everything else in his life and so he undertook a pilgrimage to visit "the places of God." Notice his language. He was "inflamed," urged on by "a sort of divine instinct," and his desire was "violent." One of the most remarkable pilgrimages, in terms of sheer numbers, is the Hajj, in which millions of Muslims converge on religious sites in Saudi Arabia at a certain time every year.

We can make a distinction between pilgrimages and tourism, which is done to satisfy curiosity, to have pleasurable experiences, to see different cultures, to spend time in spectacularly beautiful natural sites, and so on. Some tourism involves pilgrimages, which we can suggest are a kind of tourism.

Tourism is, as I see things, essentially an "id" kind of experience, based on desires we have to be entertained, escape from our routines, and that kind of thing. Pilgrimages are "superego" experiences, generated by conscience, guilt, and religious sensibilities. I distinguish between the two kinds of travels in the chart below, adapted from my book *Deconstructing Travel: Cultural Perspectives on Tourism* (Table 5.6).

Pilgrims go to holy places, to what Eliade calls "sacred" spaces, to identify with their gods, and to reinforce their religious beliefs. Tourists go to profane spaces, but often also visit sacred places, such as cathedrals, temples, and mosques, in the course of their travels. Certain cities have a sacred significance such as the Vatican City, Jerusalem, and Mecca. In these cities, historical events involving religious figures give them their significance.

Pilgrimages and travel, in general, involve the work of many people who facilitate the trips. I am talking about travel agents, tour guides, hotel clerks, bus and taxi drivers, airplane pilots and crews, cruise ship officers and crews, cooks and waiters in restaurants, and countless others. Hundreds of millions of people are going places every year, which helps explain why tourism is now the largest industry in the world.

We now turn to a particular kind of tourism that has significance for our interest in the sacred nature of tourism, namely what I describe as the paradisiacal experience many people have on cruise ships (Fig. 5.13).

Table 5.6 Pilgrimage and regular travel compared

Pilgrimage	Regular travel
Sacred space	Profane space
Religious	Secular
Faith	Pleasure, edification
Superego	Id
Reinforcement	Self-realization
Identification	Curiosity
Shrines	Sites

Fig. 5.13 *The Star Princess.* Photo by the Author

Fig. 5.14 Prime Rib Dinner on the *Star Princess.* Photo by the Author

The reason I see cruises as paradisiacal is that on these ships all of your basic needs are taken care of by the cruise line. You get three free meals a day but you can eat as much as you want at various cafeterias on the ship. You can get room service all the time.

You can arrange to have your breakfast delivered to your room if you don't want to get up and get dressed to go to one of the many restaurants and cafes on the ships that serve breakfast. And you never have any work to do—except deciding what to eat when you're dining or what excursions to take if you want to go on an excursion (Fig. 5.14).

Dining is an important element of cruising and the ships offer menus with an amazing variety of choices for every meal. Waiters and assistant waiters are trained to respond to any reasonable wish you might have and the ambiance in the dining rooms (not the cafeterias) is often quite refined.

Taking a cruise can be seen as an adventure in regression. Passengers find themselves being attended to all the time—the moral equivalent, we might say, of unconditional love. Like little children, you are prized simply for existing. Of course, you pay for this with tips, which are now collected automatically. On cruise ships, you never touch money. Your room card has your credit card number on it, so you never feel you are spending real money. You do have to pay for drinks, for dining at certain restaurants, for going to the spa for massages and other treatments, for gambling expenses, and for taking tours, but you need not do any of these things.

You pay for everything upfront and need not spend another dollar until you get on the ship. The "snake" in the garden of cruise ships is the constant and unrelenting attempt to get you to spend money on drinks, on artworks, on shoreline excursions, on wine tastings, and that kind of thing.

If you want to push things to the extreme, cruise ships can be seen as modern versions of Noah's ark, with various modifications implemented to take care of the needs of modern people. People who take cruises are not aware of the paradisiacal nature of the experience or its sacred nature. They take cruises to have fun, to visit different places effortlessly.

On a cruise ship, you are in what tourism scholars call a "first world bubble," which you can return to after visiting some site of interest. And, as the cruise lines continually remind us, you only unpack once on a cruise (Fig. 5.15).

Cruises also have an element of the carnivalesque, since cruises are devoted to pleasure and there is music, dancing, and celebrations of one kind or another all the time. M.M. Bakhtin explains what carnivalization means in his book *Rabelais and His World*. He writes (1984, pp. 7–8):

> Carnival is not a spectacle seen by the people; they live in it, and everyone participates because its very idea embraces all the people. While carnival lasts, there is no other life outside it. During carnival time life is subject only to its laws, that is, the laws of its own freedom. It has a universal spirit; it is a special condition of the entire world, of the world's revival and renewal in which all take part....it is a festive life.

It is worth noting that the largest cruise line in the world is named Carnival cruises, which owns many other cruise lines. There is a festive element to cruises that enhances the feelings of pleasure and joy in passengers.

Fig. 5.15 Mikhail Bakhtin

In the middle ages, carnival was a response to the oppressive nature of everyday life and was actually sanctioned by the church, which recognized the value of a temporary escape from the rigors of everyday life.

There are carnivalesque elements to cruises. There is music, there is lavish dining (when I've taken cruises, the evening meal usually took more than 2 h to complete), and there is drinking, along with entertainers of all kinds and even lavish theatrical shows in the theaters. It is reasonable to suggest, then, that there are sacred and what Bakhtin would describe as "carnivalesque" dimensions to cruising—even if the passengers do not recognize that this is the case.

Case Study 5: The Crying of Lot 49

Thomas Pynchon's novel, *The Crying of Lot 49* (1965), is generally considered a classic example of a postmodern novel. It is a pastiche, containing a play with a novel, and it is permeated by a fascination with American popular culture and American material culture. It is ironic in tone and has characters with fantastic names, whose significance is only meaningful to people who are familiar with American popular culture.

We can say that modernism involves stylistic purity and a belief in metanarratives; postmodernism involves stylistic eclecticism and variety, with the pastiche as the governing metaphor. A pastiche is similar to a collage, with bits and pieces of this and that forming a work of art.

If modernism believes we can know reality, postmodernism argues that we are all confounded by illusions and hyperreality. Postmodernism is the realm of consumer culture, in contrast to what we might call the production culture of modernism.

On the first page of *The Crying of Lot 49* we learn that the heroine of the story, Mrs. Oedipa Maas, has returned from a Tupperware party and has discovered that she has been named as the executor of the estate of a real estate mogul, Pierce Inverarity, with whom she had an affair before she got married to her husband, Wendell Mucho Maas. He had spent 5 years as a used car salesman and now was a disk jockey at a very small, 1000 watt, radio station, where every day was one of humiliation for him. We read, in the first paragraph of the story:

> Oedipa stood in the living room, stared at by the greenish dead eye of the TV tube, spoke the name of God, tried to feel as drunk as possible.

All through the novel, we find references to media and popular culture, such as Tupperware parties, fondue (at one time a craze in America), and other objects of daily life such as clipped grocery coupons, help wanted ads, Yellow Pages, Impala Chevrolets, TV, Muzak, and the Beatles.

We must be mindful of the names of characters, of rock groups, of towns, of radio and television stations. Of all names. Thus, for example, Oedipa's husband works at a radio station KCUF, where he attends record hops and shacks up with young girls.

Pynchon captures the southern California ambiance in his description of San Narciso (a made-up town) as a "vast sprawl of houses which had grown up all together, like a well-tended crop, from the dull brown earth." It is also smoggy out and the houses there have numbers in the thousands, like many other cities in the Los Angeles area.

She starts her quest as executor by leaving her hometown, Kinnear-Among-the-Pines, whistling a tune "I Want to Kiss Your Feet," a hit song by Sick Dick and the Volkswagens, and drives to San Narciso, a town near Los Angeles. She stays at a motel named "Echo Courts," which has a thirty-foot painting of a nymph with "a public smile, not quite a hooker's." The manager of the motel, Miles, is a sixteen-year-old (maybe) drop-out, who is a member of a band, the Paranoids, and sings one of his band's songs, in an English accent, which she overhears. Its title is "Miles' Song" and its first line is "too fat to frug." Paranoia, we will find, is a constant theme in this novel.

Oedipa has arranged a meeting with a lawyer named Metzger, from the law firm of Warpe, Wistfull, Kubitschek, and McMingus, who had written her the letter telling about Inverarity's will, which had only recently been discovered. He finds her after looking at several hotels in the area. He is carrying a bottle of wine. She had planned on watching *Bonanza*.

Metzger had been an actor named "Baby Igor," and when she turns on the television set, by chance a film with "Baby Igor" in it starts playing. So we have a curious situation in which a film with a young Metzger, as "Baby Igor" called *Cashiered*, is playing on the television set. Eventually, Oedipa and Metzger have sex, after a lot of drinking, with the Paranoids playing one of their songs; just as they climax, the lights and the television set go dark. The Paranoids had blown a fuse.

In the third chapter, we learn that many revelations were coming her way, with Inverarity's stamp collection being particularly significant. When she receives a letter with a blurb "REPORT ALL OBSCENE MAIL TO YOUR POSTMASTER," she becomes curious about what she thinks, at first, is a spelling mistake." She goes with Metzger to a strange bar, The Scope, which were electronic assembly people from Yoyodyne, a huge electronics conglomerate that was located in the area. There she meets someone named Mike Fallopian, who is a member of the Peter Pinguid Society, a right-wing society that makes the John Birch society look like it is full of left-wingers. In the toilet, Oedipa sees:

> Interested in sophisticated fun? You, hubby, girlfriends. The more the merrier. Get in touch with Kirby through WASTE only, Box 7891, L.A.

Underneath she sees a symbol of WASTE, a loop, triangle, and trapezoid. She copies the information into her memo book and leaves the toilet.

Fallopian tells her she wasn't supposed to see the notice about WASTE. He gives her an envelope, but instead of a stamp, it has the initials PPS. We are now at the beginning of the major thrust of the novel—the existence of a parallel mail system, the Tristero System, or more commonly The Tristero.

Not long after this, on a visit to Frangoso Lagoops, one of Inverarity's last major projects, they attend a play staged by the San Narciso Tank Players. This enables Pynchon to offer an eight-page parody of a medieval play called *The Courier's Tragedy* written by a seventeenth-century playwright Richard Wharfinger. The play's beginning reads as follows:

> Angelo, then, evil Duke of Squamuglia, has perhaps ten years before the play's opening murdered the good Duke of adjoining Faggio, by poisoning the feet on an image of Saint Narcissus, Bishop of Jerusalem, in the court chapel, which feet the Duke was in the habit of kissing every Sunday at Mass. This enables the evil illegitimate son, Pasquale, to take over as regent for his half-brother Niccolo, the rightful heir and good guy of the play, till he comes of age.

The fourth act ends with a poem:

> He that we last as Thurn and Taxis knew.
> Now recks no lord by the stiletto's Thorn,
> And Tacit lies the gold once-knotted horn.
> No hallowed skein of start can, ward, I trow,
> Who's once been set his tryst with Trystero.

After the fifth act, which recounts a bloodbath visited on the court of Squamiglia, which played Metzger remarked, like a Road Runner cartoon in blank verse, Oedipa goes backstage to visit the director of the play, Randolph Driblette. She wants to find out why he had his actors assume a certain face when the term "Trystero" was used.

After visits with a stamp collector named Genghis Cohen and a trip to Berkeley, she takes stock of what she knows about the Trystero. It opposed a postal system in Europe called Thurn and Taxis, its symbol was a muted post horn, it had come to America and battled with the Pony Express and Wells Fargo, and it still existed, in California, "serving as a channel for those of unorthodox sexual persuasion," including, possibly, it turns out, her husband.

She discovers, later, that there is an underworld of suiciders who failed, who keep in touch through a secret delivery system. She wanders around San Francisco and comes upon endless post horn symbols, which suggests to her that the Trystero alternative mail system is widespread.

Pynchon describes her illumination:

> For here were God knew how many citizens, deliberately choosing not to communicated by U.S. Mail. It was not an act of treason, nor possibly even of defiance. But it was a calculated withdrawal from the life of the Republic, from its machinery. Whatever else was being denied them out of hate, indifference to the

power of their vote, loopholes, simple ignorance, this withdrawal was their own, unpublicized, private.

Pynchon devotes several pages to Oedipa's adventures in Berkeley and San Francisco. At the end of her adventures there, she had verified that the WASTE system existed, had seen some WASTE postmen and WASTE stamps and cancellations.

With that accomplished, she drives back to her hometown where she discovers her therapist, Dr. Hilarius, has gone crazy and is having paranoid delusions. He pulls her into his office and she becomes a hostage. He talks about his early days at Buchenwald where he experimented on Jews. Eventually, the police break into Hilarius's office and take him away. The event is being covered by Mucho Maas for KCUF.

She ends up at the radio station where she meets the program director, Caesar Funch, who tells her that her husband hasn't been himself and every day is becoming more generic. It turns out that Mucho had been taking LSD, prescribed by Dr. Hilarius.

She goes to visit Emery Bortz, an expert on *The Courier' Tragedy*, to ask him about the lines in the production of the play she saw with the term "Trystero." He shows her slides of images from a Vatican edition of the play in which the figure of Death hovers in the background. He discusses different theories about the play:

> The moral rage, it's a throwback, it's medieval. D'Amico thinks this edition was a Scurvhamite project."
> "Scurvhamite?"
> Robert Scurvham had founded, during the reign of Charles I, a sect of most pure Puritans. Their central hang-up had to do with predestination. There were two kinds. Nothing for a Scurvhamite ever happened by accident, Creation was a vast, intricate machine. But one part of it, the Scurvhamite part, ran of the will of God, its prime mover. The rest ran off some opposite Principle, something blind, soulless; a brute automatism that led to eternal death.

Eventually, Bortz explained, they all died out and that Trystero symbolized the Other for the Puritans. He gives her a book by Wharfinger about someone named Diocletian Blobb and then Blobb's commonplace book, *Peregrinations*.

He recounts how he was traveling with his servant in a desolate area in a mail coach belonging to Thurn and Taxis when they were set upon by a group of black-cloaked riders who collected the mail sacks that were being carried and killed everyone except Blobb. The leader of the brigands gives Blobb a message to bring back to England:

> Tell your king and parliament what we have done. Tell them that we prevail. That neither tempest nor strife, nor fierce beasts, nor the loneliness of the desert, nor yet the illegitimate usurpers of our rightful estate, can deter our couriers.

Oedipa pieces together the way the Trystero began. A central figure in the story is Hernando Joaquin de Tristero y Calavera, "perhaps a madman, perhaps an honest rebel, who battled with his cousin over control of the mail service." Tristero set up his own mail service whose theme involved the disinherited. He chose a uniform of black for his followers and a muted post horn for his symbol. He began a campaign of terrorizing and disrupting the Thurn and Taxis mail routes.

She discovers that every aspect of the Trystero was connected with the Inverarity estate, which made her question whether she'd stumbled into a secret society operating in America and sending mail in a parallel mail service or Inverarity hatched a plot to make Oedipa think she had discovered a secret society that didn't exist.

One day she gets a call from Genghis Cohen, who informs her that the Trystero forgeries were to be sold at auction, as lot 49. She goes with Cohen to the auction and as the auctioneer is clearing his throat, ready to announce Lot 49, the book ends.

Oedipa learns that what she thought she was doing, making sense of Inverarity's legacy, was only part of the story. Pynchon writes "She had dedicated herself, weeks ago, to making sense of what Inverarity had left behind, never suspecting that the legacy was America." *The Crying of Lot 49* is a quintessentially American novel, grounded in American popular culture and full of people with strange names and preoccupations.

It is a brilliant satire of an America of high school rock bands, right-wing politicians, little lookalike boxes of houses in which people in southern California live, of nutcase therapists, of LSD takers, of everyday life, and the weird people one finds, if you scratch beneath the surface, everywhere in America.

The mystery Oedipa sets out to solve is similar to the quests that religious people have in search of the mysteries of life and their gods. *The Chicago Times* described it as "Pynchon's version of the Holy Grail," which suggests that there is a sacred nature to Oedipa's quest.

Richard Poirier's review of *The Crying of Lot 49* in *The New York Times* (1965) offers us an insight into the novel's larger cultural significance. He writes in an essay titled "Embattled Underground" (May 1, 1966):

> This novel is a patriotic lamentation, an elaborate effort not to believe the worst about the Republic. Patriotism for an ideal of America explains the otherwise yawning gap in Pynchon's comic shaping of his material. The Tristero System--it began in 1577 in Holland in opposition to the Thurn and Taxis Postal System and is active now in America trying to subvert the American postal system through an organization called W.A.S.T.E.--is a masterpiece of comic invention. It involves, among other things, one of the best parodies ever written of Jacobean drama, "The Courier's Tragedy," and a perhaps final parody of California right-wing organizations, Peter Pequid Society, named for the commanding officer of the Confederate man-of-war "Disgruntled" and opposed to industrial capitalism

on the grounds that it has led inevitably to Marxism. Its leader, Mike Fallopian, speculates in California real estate.

Readers of *The Crying of Lot 49* may think they are finding out about the Tystero system but, in reality, they are finding out about America.

References

Adler, Elkan Nathan. 1930. *Jewish travelers*. London: Routledge.
Bakhtin, Mikhail. 1984. *Rabelais and his world*. Bloomington: Indiana University Press.
Belk, Russel W., Melanie Wllendorf, and John F. Sherry. 1989. The Sacred and the Profane in consumer behavior: Theodicy and The Odyssey. *Journal of Consumer Behavior*. 16 (1): 1–38.
Berger, Arthur Asa. 2019. *Media analysis techniques*. 6th ed. Thousand Oaks, CA: Sage.
Biderman, David. 2010, January 15. Football games have 11 minutes of action. *The Wall Street Journal*.
Brooker, Peter. 1999. *Cultural theory: A glossary*. London: Arnold.
Dichter, Ernest. 1960. *The strategy of desire*. Garden City, NY: Doubleday.
Durkheim, Emile. 1965. *The elementary forms of the religious life*. New York, NY: Free Press.
Eliade, Mircea. 1961. *The sacred and the Profane: The nature of religion*. New York, NY: Harper & Row.
Haug, Wolfgang. 1986. *Critique of commodity aesthetics: Appearance, sexuality, and advertising in capitalist society*. Minneapolis: University of Minnesota Press.
Henderson, Joseph L. 1968. Ancient myths and modern man. In *Man and his symbols*, ed. Carl G. Jung. Garden City, NY: Doubleday.
Huizinga, Johan. 1924. *The waning of the middle ages*. Garden City, NY: Anchor.
Lyotard, Jean-François. 1984. *The postmodern condition: A report on knowledge*. Minneapolis: University of Minnesota Press.
Poirier, Richard. 1966, May 1. Embattled underground. *The New York Times*.
Pynchon, Thomas. 1965. *The crying of lot 49*. Philadelphia, PA: J. B. Lippincott & Co.

PART II

My Contributions to the Study of Everyday Life

CHAPTER 6

My Contributions to Analyzing Everyday Life and Postmodernism: From a Cultural Studies Perspective

Chapter Objectives This chapter offers a dozen short selections from articles and books by the author that deal with postmodernism, everyday life, and related concerns. They are used to show how cultural studies and its four main disciplines, semiotics, psychoanalytic theory, Marxism, and sociological theory, can be used to analyze everything from material culture (Echo Dots and blue jeans) to tourism, myths, and architecture. The topics covered in this chapter are McDonald's hamburgers, a book on American material culture titled *Bloom's Morning*, a novel *Postmortem for a Postmodernist*, the Amazon Echo Dot, a video game called *Pac-Man*, postmodern elements in a tourist destination, Bali, a Sherlock Holmes novel by the author, a book on Trump, the ideas of a French sociologist Jean Baudrillard on hyperreality, a model using myth devised by the author, Erich Fromm's thought, and a study of Las Vegas architecture.

Keywords Postmodernism • Everyday life • Semiotics • Psychoanalytic theory • Marxism • Sociological theory

> America is neither dream nor reality. It is a hyperreality....Everything here is real and pragmatic, and yet is the stuff of dreams too. It may be that the truth of America can only be seen by a European, since he alone will discover here the perfect simulacrum—that of the immanence and material transcription of all values. The Americans, for their part, have no sense of simulation. They are themselves simulation in its most developed state, but they have no language in which to describe it, since they themselves are the model.

> Jean Baudrillard, *America*. London: Verso. 1988.

> The postmodernists have, in fact, been fascinated precisely by this whole "degraded" landscape of schlock and kitsch, of TV series and *Reader's Digest* culture, of advertising and motels, of the late show and grade-B Hollywood film, of so-called paraliterature, with its airport categories of the gothic and the romance, the popular biography, the murder mystery and the science fiction or fantasy novel.... (1991, p. 2)

> Fredric Jameson, *Postmodernism or, The Cultural Logic of Late Capitalism*. Durham, North Carolina: Duke University Press. 1991.

> For the semiotician, the contradictory nature of the American myth of equality is nowhere written so clearly as in the signs that American advertisers use to manipulate us into buying their wares. "Manipulate" is the word here, not "persuade"; for advertising campaigns are not sources of product information, they are exercises in behavior modification. Appealing to our subconscious emotions rather than to our conscious intellects, advertisements are designed to exploit the discontentment fostered by the American dream, the constant desire for social success and the material rewards that accompany it. America's consumer economy runs on desire, and advertising stokes the engines by transforming common objects—from peanut butter to political candidates—into signs of all the things that Americans covet most.

> Jack Solomon, *The Signs of Our Times: The Secret Meanings of Everyday Life*. New York: Perennial. 1990.

Since I've been writing about everyday life in America from a cultural studies perspective, since 1965 when I wrote my Ph.D. dissertation in American Studies on a comic strip, I've analyzed many different subjects. I will share some of my writings in relatively brief excerpts that I hope you will find illuminating and interesting and an example of how cultural studies can be applied to topics of one kind or another. None of the quoted material is longer than 350 words, because of copyright prohibitions, except for those which come from books for which I own the copyright and are a few hundred words longer (Fig. 6.1).

Fig. 6.1 McDonald's. Photo by the author

McDonald's "Evangelical" Hamburgers

The Minnesota Daily, 1965

> McDonald's offers a hamburger without qualities for the man without qualities. It must be seen as more than a gaudy, vulgar oasis of tasteless ground meat, a fountain of sweet, syrupy malted milks in a big parking lot that caters to insolvent students, snack seekers, and hard-up hungers who grind its bloody gristle through their choppers at fifteen cents a shot. No! McDonald's is not just a hamburger joint….it is America, or, rather, it is the supreme triumph of all that is insane in American life.
>
> At McDonald's there is no human touch…just little packets of wrapped hamburgers, sacks of fried potatoes—everything is packed in little bags to be thrown away. Is there any pleasure connected with eating a McDonald's hamburger? I think not! The only relief you have is that it didn't cost sixteen cents or even twenty cents. It only costs fifteen cents because American technology and free enterprise have dictated that an automated hamburger is worth only fifteen cents.

I wrote this essay, published under the title "The Evangelical Hamburger," full of purple prose and dire warnings, in 1965, after I had eaten my first McDonald's hamburger. There had been an empty lot I often passed when walking to my office at the University of Minnesota, where I taught lower-division courses in English. One day when I passed the lot I saw a small, white, building with huge yellow arches and an electronic sign, full of rapidly rising numbers, indicating the number of people who had eaten McDonald's hamburgers.

It struck me that the arches had a religious significance to them and the electronic sign indicated that people who ate a McDonald's hamburger were members of a community…or, even stronger, a congregation. And the way one ordered a hamburger seemed very structured or, in effect, a ritual. The fifteen cents could be construed as an offering to the new religion. I recognized then that McDonald's would spread, with "evangelical" fervor, all through America and the world.

The McDonald's hamburger, only fifteen cents, was a symbol, for me, of the forces of mechanization and standardization that, I felt, were to dominate American culture and society.

* * *

Bloom's Morning: Coffee, Comforters, and the Secret Meaning of Everyday Life

I began my discussion of everyday life in America with a discussion of digital clock radios. It was the first of 36 short essays I wrote on various objects and rituals that are part of American everyday life.

> The digital clock merely produces numbers that locate us in the immediate present but it also, at the same time, disconnects us from the past and the future. A digital clock destroys time as we traditionally think of it; time is dissolved into an endless succession of discrete and unrelated moments.
>
> This dissolution of time, the radical separation of an instant of time from both time past and time future, can be looked upon as a metaphor for the alienation many people feel, in contemporary society. Our electronic culture gives us precision at the cost of community and a sense of relatedness. Thus digital clocks are objects which reflect, it can be argued, the alienation which many people now feel. These clocks are both symptoms of this alienation and perpetrators of it, for their very accuracy is, in certain respects, upsetting and in some ways even dehumanizing.
>
> Clocks are, we must remember, whatever else they may be, instruments of control. We lived for centuries without them. The first clocks appeared in the 13th Century; minute hands appeared in the 17th Century (with the invention of the pendulum) and the second hand had to wait until the 18th century. These early clocks revolutionized people's lives... until the development of clocks, it was not possible to regulate the way people spent their time with very much accuracy. The clock made possible the development of the industrial era. People learned, eventually, that "time is money." Given this, time suddenly becomes a precious commodity.
>
> And the more accuracy we have at our command, the better things are—as far as utilizing clocks as instruments of control is concerned. To be middle-class means, among other things, to be socialized into getting places on time, into internalizing the correct attitude towards time.

My book *Bloom's Morning* was originally titled Ulysses Sociological America and was an attempt to deal with the everyday life of a typical American, Bloom, the same way that James Joyce did with his hero, Leopold Bloom. I found it so difficult to analyze the various things Bloom did that I decided to only do his morning.

* * *

Fig. 6.2 *Postmortem for a Postmodernist* cover

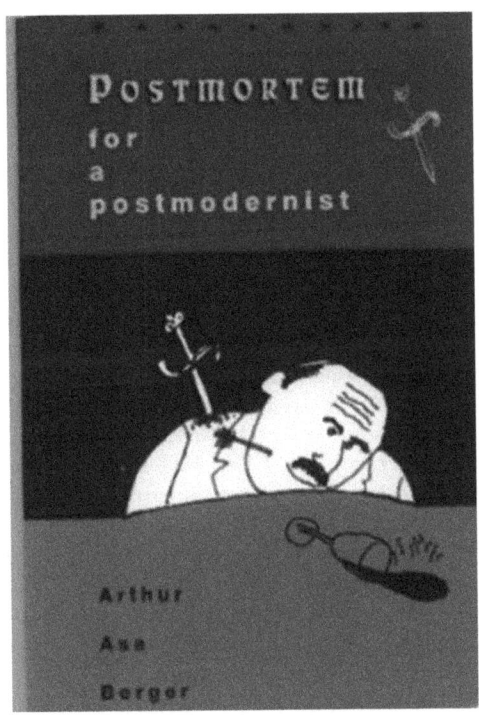

Postmortem for a Postmodernist

This book is a mystery novel about postmodernism that has been translated into Chinese, Indonesian, Turkish, and probably several other languages. In many countries, publishers don't bother getting permission from the publisher and translate books as they see fit. In my novel, the victim, a semiotics professor named Ettore Gnocchi, is killed four different ways on the first page (Fig. 6.2).

A detective, Solomon Hunter, is sent to the scene of the crime and interviews everyone at Gnocchi's home, where he was killed. They were all at a dinner party. Shoshana TelAviv, Gnocchi's wife, is the first person Hunter interviews and he is, as might be expected, curious about what postmodernism is when he is told that Gnocchi was a famous postmodernist thinker.

For some reason, this novel is very popular in China and when I was there for a lecture at a university recently, one of the members of my audience asked me about it.

> "I've heard that term before," said Hunter. "What exactly is postmodernism?"
> Shoshana TelAviv smiled, weakly.
> "It's not a simple matter. Ettore has written a dozen books on the subject, and I've written a couple on it as well. You might find it more instructive to look at them. In a word or two, postmodernism refers to the general contours of our culture for the last fifty years, give or take a decade. Or so many people argue."

She paused for a moment. "If you want to understand why American society is the way it is, you have to understand postmodernism and the influence it has had."

"Do you mean it's a philosophy? Or an economic system? Or an art style?" asked Hunter.

"Not at all. Postmodernism refers to what might be called a condition or theory, a collection of beliefs and values, and attitudes that, though we might not realize it, shape our consciousness and our society. We find it the way we mix up different styles and genres in the arts and architecture. But it's not just an aesthetic...it's a way of understanding the world and of living...though most of the people whose lives have been shaped...or perhaps affected is a better term...by postmodernism have never heard of the term. "Maybe this will help," she said. "One of the leading postmodernist thinkers, the late French scholar Michel Foucault, was what might be called a perspectivist. Foucault pointed out that we don't live in a world of facts that have a meaning independent of people but, instead, in a world constantly subject to our ever-changing interpretations of it. There are many different interpretations of phenomena and, as the German philosopher Friedrich Nietzsche argued, there's no limit to the ways in which the world can be interpreted. So the more perspectives we have on anything, the more profound our knowledge and our understanding of it will be. Thus postmodernism, in opposing unified and simplistic views of life and history, has in subtle ways shaped our contemporary consciousness."

This academic mystery novel is also, in my mind, a textbook that uses a narrative genre, the detective story, to engage readers and teach them something about postmodernism.

* * *

The Amazon Echo Dot

I am interested in new technologies and so when the Amazon Echo Dot appeared and was on sale, I purchased one. Because I live in a house on a hill, the part of my house on the downward slope has three floors and, on the bottom floor, my wife has her study. To communicate with her, I bought an Echo Dot for her study and one for our bedroom, on the second floor.

It turns out that the Google smart speaker has a better search engine than Amazon, so I bought an Amazon smart speaker for my study and one for my library. Then, my son gave me an Amazon Face with a five-inch screen for my library. Just recently, my daughter gave me a seven-inch Google Nest Hub (second generation).

So, one way or another, we now have eight smart speakers in the house—one or more for every room except the laundry room. The six smart speakers I bought cost around $19 each so for around $120, I've wired my house. (The two smart speakers with screens cost around $50 each.) I might add that I recently purchased a "smart" television set that takes commands from Alexa.

Fig. 6.3 The Amazon Echo Dot

What follows is a discussion of this device found in my book, *Perspectives on Everyday Life: A Cross Disciplinary Analysis* (Fig. 6.3).

In my mind, smart speakers are signifiers of the way what I describe as the "electronic imperative" has insinuated itself, if not taken control, of postmodern societies. I offer in this passage a psychoanalytic interpretation of the hidden or unconscious significance of these devices.

> The Amazon Echo Dot is the most important new genre (or product category) of electronic devices since the smartphone and its offshoot, the tablet. Like the smartphone, the Echo Dot is a multi-functional device, except that instead of using "apps" it continually is taught new things—what it calls "skills" that it can do. The Echo smart speaker was invented by Amazon.com, which is now a major technology company as well as a retailing giant. Other companies, most notably Google with its Home speakers, are now competing with Amazon in the smart speaker business. By 2022, it is estimated by Forrester research that more than 66 million American households, or approximately 172 million people, will have these devices.
>
> Functionality of the Echo Dot and Smart Speakers
>
> We don't know how many new things the Dot or its competitors such as the Google Home Mini will eventually be able to do, but the Echo Dot's list of skills is considerable…and growing every week as programmers figure out how to teach Alexa to do new things. Currently it has around fifteen thousand "skills" but there's no knowing how many it will eventually have. Alexa can play the sound of waves to soothe us, can help us meditate, can provide us with the news whenever we want it, and can wake us up in the morning with a loud alarm.
>
> The Power of Speech
>
> What is basic to all these devices is that they are based on speech to control then—on the enabling power of our words to do certain things. We can use our speech to interact with people, and with dogs and other animals, but we've never been able to use speech to control electronic devices and interact with them so easily. I've read stories about elderly people living alone who have found ways to interact with smart speakers such as the Echo Dot or the Google Home Mini, and assuage their loneliness. At the unconscious level, our ability to command Alexa and the nameless speaker on the Google Home Mini provides us with a sense of agency and power.

The meaning and cultural significance of these devices are not apparent to most people and are not strictly a matter of their functionality. The objects that are important in our everyday lives have hidden meanings of which most people are unaware. Somehow, for one reason or another, I now have four Amazon Dots, one five-inch Amazon Home with a screen (a gift), one seven-inch Google Nest Hub with a screen, and two Google Home Minis.

* * *

"Pac-Man"

My article on "Pac-Man" appeared in the *Los Angeles Times* in 1984 (or maybe 1983) and generated many letters questioning my sanity. These letters were from people, I would imagine, with little knowledge of semiotics or psychoanalytic theory.

The video game industry is now larger than the film industry and is growing all the time, with new and powerful devices for playing video games coming onto the market now. My two grandsons are obsessed with video games and told me about their newest fixation, "Among Us." I watched some people playing this game on YouTube and it seemed to be pretty moronic, but I am not an adolescent with, to my mind, unrefined tastes.

Here is my analysis of "Pac-Man," in which I argue that the game reveals that a significant change has taken place in the American psyche.

> Earlier video games (and the video game phenomenon is significant in its own right) such as "Space Invaders" and so on, involved rocket ships coursing through outer space, blasting aliens and hostile forces with ray guns, laser beams, and other weapons, and represented a very different orientation from "Pac Man." The games were highly phallic and they also expressed a sense of freedom and openness. The games were played in outer space and one had a sense of infinite possibility.
>
> "Pac-Man," however, represents something quite different. The game takes place in a labyrinth which implies, metaphorically, that we are all trapped, closeted in a claustrophobic situation in which the nature of things is that we must either eat or be eaten. This oral aspect of the game suggests further that there is some kind of diffuse regression taking place and we have moved from the phallic stage (guns, rockets) to the oral stage (eating, biting).

This analysis of "Pac-Man" relies on psychoanalytic theory and applies many concepts from that theory to the video game. Things have changed considerably from 1984 when I wrote the article, and video games now often have incredible graphics and have become very immersive (perhaps dangerously so) narratives (Fig. 6.4).

* * *

Fig. 6.4 Bali dance scene

Is Bali Postmodern?

In my book, *Bali Tourism*, I deal in some depth with Bali, which is an important tourism destination, and with Balinese culture, which is extremely interesting. I argue that though it may seem a stretch, Balinese culture is postmodern.

> It might seem to suggest that a so-called "exotic" third-world culture, like the one we find in Bali, might also be postmodern. A postmodern Bali sounds like an oxymoron. The term postmodern has to do with periodization, and so we assume that you can only have a postmodern society after you have a modern one, which means a so-called traditional society, such as is found in Bali, has to become a modern one before it can become a postmodern one. It may be, however, that we can find postmodern societies in places such as Bali.
>
> One of the basic aspects of the postmodern involves the pastiche, a mixture of different kinds of elements in some entity, and with simulations and a lack of concern with that which is "authentic." The postmodern is also identified with a lack of belief in overarching and universal philosophical principles. On all of these counts I think it is reasonable to suggest that Bali is postmodern, and tourism was probably the agent that led to Bali achieving its postmodernity.
>
> For one thing, there is a great deal of eclecticism in Bali. Some people, in villages that are not frequented by tourists, lead the kind of lives that the Balinese have always led, though they have access to the new media, and that is a force for change. But other villages, where tourists frequent, have interesting combinations of contemporary consumer cultures and Balinese ceremonial religious cultures.
>
> The Balinese form of Hinduism is, Geertz suggests, non-theological and is focused on a seemingly endless series of ceremonies tied to the large number of Hindu temples found on the island. The Balinese, if Geertz is correct, are not interested in theology but in religious practices, and that seems quite postmodern. In addition, the modified and adapted forms of dance and other kinds of artistic expression in Bali can be construed as "simulations" of sorts, suggesting something of the postmodern in them.

Fig. 6.5 Sherlock Holmes

Daniel Boorstin, a well-known cultural theorist, attacked Bali's adapted forms of artistic expression as "impure," but in my opinion, it makes sense to tailor one's arts to one's audience. The best, which can be described as Bali's traditional forms of dance and music and artistic expression that Boorstin favors, is the enemy of the good—namely that which tourists can assimilate and appreciate.

Boorstin is a modernist and there is a strong tinge of the elitist about his writing on tourism and its so-called pseudo-experiences. Reading his book *The Image: A Guide to Pseudo-Events in America* (and by implication elsewhere in the world) I can't help but think that he makes the same arguments about tourism that critics, over many decades, have made about popular culture and the mass media (Fig. 6.5).

* * *

My Name Is Sherlock Holmes: Sherlock Holmes is Introduced to Cultural Theory

In this book, Sherlock Holmes is involved in a case in which he interviews various writers and theorists who have come to London for a conference on the roots of behavior. I offer here some material from Holmes' interview with Ferdinand de Saussure, one of the founding fathers of semiotics, the science of signs. In this book, the story is written in the first person, with Holmes as the narrator. Much of Saussure's dialogue is taken from his book.

> "I am a linguistic professor who has developed a branch of linguistics I call semiology. I believe this science will play an increasingly important role in all the social sciences and humanities, as well," said Saussure.

"Oh," I said. "A linguistics professor. That's a bit of a surprise. I guess there are scholars from many different disciplines at the conference."

"Let me explain something about semiology," he replied. My first insight was that language is a self-contained system in which the parts are all interdependent and acquire value and meaning through their relationships to the whole. Words are signs. So are objects. Semiologists are interested in all forms of expression since everything conveys meaning to people. But how does this transmission of meaning work? Through language and images, generally. I make a distinction between speaking and language. Speaking is an individual act and is based on the way a speaker uses words provided to the speaker by language, which is a social institution."

"Very interesting," I replied.

"Good," said Saussure. "I argue that language is a system of signs that express ideas and is therefore similar to writing, symbolic rites, military signals, and polite formulas, but it is the most important of these systems. A science that studies the life of signs in society is conceivable. I call it semiology, from the Greek term sēmeîon. Semiology shows us what constitutes a sign and what laws govern them. In my theory, a sign unites not a thing and a name but a sound-image and a concept. I call the sound-image a signifier and the concept generated by the sound-image a signified. We must remember that the relationship that exists between a signifier and a signified is arbitrary. We could have easily named what we call a tree something else. This use of signifier and signified has the advantage of indicating the opposition that separates them from each other and from the whole of which they are parts."

"Remarkable," I replied. "You've described a complicated science but implied in your description I get the feeling that, in a sense, we are all, without knowing it, semioticians."

"Precisely," said Saussure. "But there is a bit more to explain. I've already said that language is a system of interdependent terms in which the meaning of each term results from the simultaneous presence of other terms. So it is relationships that are basic."

"That makes sense to me," I said.

"When we come to concepts, we find that their meaning is purely differential and defined not by their positive content but negatively by their relations with the other terms of the system, so their most precise characteristic is in being what the others are not. I know that this is a mouthful, but we must realize that signs function, not through their intrinsic value but through their relative position. Thus, in language there are only differences, and language is based on oppositions. For example, a sentence has meaning only through its parts and the parts have value due to their place on the whole. In language, it is relationships that are basic, and the most important relationship is binary opposition: rich and poor, happy and sad, and, at one time, male and female."

This book is one of half a dozen academic mysteries I have written that are also textbooks. In the dialogue in my mysteries, some of the material comes from the writings of the theorists that Holmes or my other detective, Solomon Hunter, interviews.

* * *

Fig. 6.6 Trump balloon

THREE TROPES ON TRUMP (FIG. 6.6)

In my book on Trump, the three "tropes" I used to analyze him were semiotics, psychoanalytic theory, and Marxist theory. I argue that it is possible to understand trump as a postmodern president.

> What Trump did was to capitalize on the discontent and rage that possessed huge numbers of the people and on the sense of reality that had been fractured by postmodern society and the media in a postmodern America. Jean-Francois Lyotard, a French scholar, has characterized postmodernism as "incredulity toward metanarratives" in his book *The Postmodern Condition* (1984, p. xxiv). As he explained: Simplifying to the extreme, I define postmodernism as incredulity toward narratives….To the obsolescence of the metanarrative apparatus of legitimation corresponds, most notably, the crisis of metaphysical philosophy and of the university institution which in the past relied on it."
>
> In postmodern society, people don't accept the old modernist overarching philosophical systems found in religion, philosophy, and other institutions which helped them make sense of the world. The grand narratives such as a belief in progress and science that the angry and dispossessed Trump voters opposed was that of traditional liberalism and rationality, as exemplified in the presidency of Barrack Obama. The problem is in postmodern society we lack a way of determining legitimacy in many areas and are, more or less, left to our own devices to determine what is right and wrong. We might suggest that Trump is our first postmodern president in the sense that he is an exemplar of the fractured self (among his other psychological problems) that is a cultural dominant in postmodern society along with the all-important role of the media. Postmodernism breaks down the distinction between elite culture and popular culture and Trump, it would seem, is someone who revels in popular or mass-mediated culture and

has no elite culture. Pundits question whether Trump has read a book in the last thirty years and he has not invited any elite culture artists to perform in the White House, unlike all recent presidents. Postmodernism can be described as a cultural mutation that became dominant around 1960 and replaced the prevailing ethos which we can describe as modernism.

Politicians, generally speaking, are modernists who believe in the power of reason and logic. Trump, I argue, is a creature of pop culture and the postmodernist ethos which doesn't differentiate between elite culture and pop culture and which disregards many of the core cultural beliefs and rules of behavior that most people follow.

In another book I wrote, on Trump's followers, I argue that they are what sociologists describe as "working-class authoritarians," and see themselves in him. I also argue that Trump is a cult leader. His loss to Joe Biden in the 2020 election was held by huge numbers of Americans as an escape from authoritarianism and fascism. Trump's acceptance, by huge numbers of Americans, is a reflection of the split in American politics between Democrats and Republicans and democracy and authoritarianism.

* * *

Jean Baudrillard and the End of History
In my book, *The Portable Postmodernist,* I offer quotations from fifty postmodernist thinkers and commentaries on each text I've used. Baudrillard is an important thinker whose ideas have been very influential. His article, "On Nihilism," is the work that I dealt with in the analysis that follows. In his article, he writes "Post-modernity is neither optimistic nor pessimistic. It is a game with the vestiges of what has been destroyed," by which he means we are living in a post-history world that is without meaning."

> Jean Baudrillard takes a historical approach to postmodernism here…and sees postmodernism as an attempt to salvage some kind of a tolerable existence out of the remnants of modernism and of history. One of the great "metanarratives" that sustained us—the idea of progress—has been tossed, he suggests, into the ash heap of history. We've gone as far as we can go, Baudrillard asserts, and history, as we know it, has come to an end. Postmodernism represents, then, the "real" game of Survivor in a world where everything has, so it seems, been emptied of meaning. Baudrillard's ideas may help explain why Survivor and other "reality" shows on television have been such big hits—we all recognize, subconsciously, that the roles of the characters in these shows are the roles we are forced to take in the new postmodern era, so there is incredible resonance, in audiences, with these programs. Isn't there something odd about the notion of having "reality" programming on television? Not if you're living in a postmodern world, one might answer. But would this answer be correct? In a postmodern world, such as that described by Baudrillard, would that matter?

After reading this passage, one can understand why it was possible for a reality show host, Donald J. Trump, to become the president of the USA and usher in a post-truth administration full of alternate realities and his "Big Lie" about not losing the 2020 election.

* * *

The Myth Model and Everyday Life
In my discussion of myths, I explain that they play an important role in our lives, even though we do not recognize this to be the case. Raphael Patai, in his book *Myth and Modern Man,* defines myth as follows:

> Myth…is a traditional religious charter, which operates by validating laws, customs, rites, institutions, and beliefs, or explaining socio-cultural situations and natural phenomena, and taking the form of stories, believed to be true, about divine beings and heroes…. Myths are dramatic stories that form a sacred charter either authorizing the continuance of ancient institutions, customs, rites, and beliefs in the area where they are current or approving alterations.

From his definition, we can understand why myths are important. That is because they "validate" so many aspects of our everyday lives. I developed what I call a "myth model" that shows how myths inform many aspects of culture and thus affect, in profound ways, our everyday lives.

We don't recognize the role myths play in our lives because they are camouflaged and function in what we might describe as a cultural subconscious, below our level of consciousness. What follows is material found in my book *Media, Myth, and Society* (2013b, p. 14):

The Myth Model
A myth, defined as a sacred narrative that validates cultural beliefs and practices
Psychoanalytic reflections of the myth
(when we can find them)
Historical manifestations of that myth
(when we can find them)
The myth in elite culture
(operas, theatre, serious novels, etc.)
The myth in mass-mediated or popular culture
(songs, advertisements, fashion, films, TV shows, etc.)
The myth in everyday life
(when we can recognize it)

In my book, I offer many examples of culturally resonant myths, such as the myth of Oedipus, the myth of Adam and Eve in the Garden of Eden, the myth of Sisyphus, the myth of Narcissus, and any number of other classical myths. I am defining myth here as a sacred story, not as an "erroneous belief," which is a different way of using the term. I offer now an example of the myth model as it involves our passion for blue jeans.

The Myth Model and Blue Jeans

Myth/Sacred Story
   Story of Joseph and his Coat of Many Colors from Bible
   "Now Israel loved Joseph more than all his children because he was the son of his old age: and he made him a coat of many colours." Genesis 37:3
   Psychoanalytic Manifestation
   Superiority feelings in Joseph, envy in his brothers. Also wearing tight blue jeans to display the rear end as a means of sexual display.
   Historical Experience
   Levi-Strauss sets up factory in California
   Elite Culture
   Ian Berry's paintings are made of blue jeans.
   Popular Culture
   Advertisements for Blue Jeans, Dolly Parton song, "Coat of Many Colors."
   Everyday Life
   Purchase a pair of blue jeans.

From this discussion, I think you can see how myths can shape many of our decisions and actions. We may not be conscious of the role of myths in our everyday lives, but as Freud pointed out, we are not conscious of most of what is in our minds (Fig. 6.7).

* * *

Fig. 6.7 Erich Fromm

Erich Fromm on Marxism and Psychoanalysis

The passage that follows is taken from my academic mystery/textbook *Marx Est Mort*. In this book, Sherlock Holmes interviews some prominent Marxist writers, both real and imagined to solve a murder mystery.

Erich Fromm wrote a book *Beyond the Chain of Illusion: My Encounter with Marx and Freud,* which explores the ideas of both men and is an important contribution to understanding the importance of both of these thinkers. I start with Fromm discussing Marxism.

> "Marx was interested in the way the dominant ideas in a society shape people's thinking and argued that the socio-economic structure of society, what he called the base, shaped the institutions and beliefs found in societies, and generated illusions in people about themselves and their possibilities. He described this as false consciousness. Freud was also interested in illusions but argued they were shaped by forces in people's unconscious that they didn't recognize. So he wanted to make the unconscious conscious and help individuals deal with their problems, passions, irrational forces, and complexes. This leads to the notion that different groups, classes, and nations have distinctive character structures, what I describe as social character, that shapes both the societies and the individuals living in that society."
>
> "Am I correct, then," Holmes interjected, that Marx believed that the economic bases of a society shape the social character of that society which then affects the ideas, beliefs, values, what you will, of people in that society, or nation if we extend it, as you have explained things?"
>
> "Yes, precisely, Mr. Holmes," replied Fromm. "From Freud's perspective, a man might believe he has the freedom to think and act as he pleases, but in reality, he is moved, like a marionette, by strings behind and above him which are in turn directed by unconscious forces in his psyche. To provide himself with the illusion that he behaves the way he does, he rationalizes his activities to make it seem like he knows why he acts the way he does. So we act under the illusions that our actions are based on free will or reason and we need to gain access to the unconscious forces that are shaping our behavior."
>
> "So how do you help people behave more rationally?" asked Dr. Watson."
>
> "There are two answers to your question. For Freud, it is to help the individual deal with the individual unconscious and the repression of instinctive forces. The focus, for all practical purposes, is on the disturbed individual. These individuals suffer from a general malaise—from a lack of satisfaction from their work, from a lack of happiness with their marriages, from a feeling they have not lived up to their potentials, and countless other maladies. They are sad and without joy, even though many of them are affluent. What many psychologists and psychoanalysts offer them is adjustment, which I would describe as an individual being as unhappy as everyone else in his society. Marx, on the other hand, advocated making structural changes in society to help everyone deal with their problems of alienation and general unhappiness. If you fix the society in which disturbed individuals live, they will be fixed, but this doesn't involve the kind of socialism that doctrinaire Marxists have advocated but a humanistic form that liberates our possibilities."

"I take it, then, that you feel that if you can psychoanalyze societies and deal with the unconscious imperatives found in a given society, or even nation, you will be making an important contribution to everyone's well-being," said Holmes.

"Precisely," said Fromm. "Why work on individual psyches when you can create a society that enables people to solve their problems due to the help the institutions of that society provide for them. As Marx put it, 'the demand to give up the illusions about its condition is the demand to give a condition which needs illusions.'"

Fromm sees Marx as a humanist rather than a revolutionary, whose ideas about the destructive nature of the alienation generated by Capitalist societies were more important than his ideas about the need for a revolution. Fromm's notion that one can psychoanalyze societies, as well as individuals, had shaped much of my thinking.

* * *

Learning from Las Vegas

Las Vegas is the second most important tourist destination in the USA (Times Square is first). It is generally held to be an excellent example of a postmodern city, based on its urban design and the architecture of the hotels that are found in the city—many built by gangsters with dubious aesthetic sensibilities.

Robert Venturi, Steven Izenour, and Denise Scott Brown wrote an influential book, *Learning from Las Vegas* that deals with the chaotic nature of the commercial strip in Las Vegas and its innovative urban design features. Las Vegas has a lot to teach architects and urbanists, but it is a city devoted to gambling (now called "gaming" to give itself a bit of respectability) and entertainment. It also prides itself on keeping its dirty secrets since it promises, "What happens in Las Vegas stays in Las Vegas."

The material that follows comes from my 2013 book, *Theorizing Tourism: Analyzing Iconic Destinations* (1972, p. 20):

> For those who want a bit of sophistication and "class," it has a hotel complex, Paris-Las Vegas, which features a half-sized version—about 500 feet high or forty stories—of the Eiffel Tower. In a sense, Las Vegas allows visitors there to be "world tourists, in that they can visit many important tourist sites and buildings, in scaled-down imitations, in one place. They can see the Sphinx, Times Square, and the Eiffel Tower in one afternoon. These simulations remind us that authenticity doesn't mean much for postmodern tourists, who want to be amused and entertained and don't care whether the sites they visit are authentic or simulations. Las Vegas becomes, then, a pastiche-like collection of world-class tourist sites that are all jumbled together in various themed hotels there. The pastiche, postmodern thinkers remind us, is the basic postmodern art form. By using themed hotels (Egypt, Paris, etc.) the companies that built these hotels were able to differentiate

themselves from other hotels on the strip and develop a distinctive identity. These themed hotels also benefitted from the auras of the places they imitated and from what we might describe as the "halo" effect provided by the imitated tourist destinations.

Why settle for the real thing, and all the expense involved in traveling to Paris or Egypt, we may ask as postmodernist tourists, when you can have the imitation and it doesn't cost very much to see—unless, that is, you develop a fondness for slot machines?

What I suggest in my analysis of the city is that its aesthetic qualities, especially as reflected in the city's many hotels, are an important factor in its success as a tourist site, in addition to the fact that it allows gaming.

* * *

With this, I bring my chapter on my contributions of a cultural studies perspective to the study of everyday life and postmodernism to an end. I have tried to suggest, in the different selections I have offered, something about the many different aspects of these topics that might be studied and about the methods for studying them.

References

Baudrillard, Jean. 1988. *America*. London: Verso.
Berger, Arthur Asa. 1965. McDonald's "Evangelical" Hamburgers. *Minnesota Daily*.
———. (1984) Pac-Man. *Los Angeles Times*.
———. 1988. *Media USA*. 2nd ed. New York: Longman.
———. 1997a. *Bloom's morning: Coffee, comforters, and the secret meaning of everyday life*. Boulder, CO: Westview Press.
———. 1997b. *Postmortem for a Postmodernist*. Walnut Creek, CA: Altamira Press.
———. 1998. *Perspectives on everyday life: A cross-disciplinary analysis*. New York: Palgrave.
———. 2003. *The portable postmodernist*. Walnut Creek, CA: Altamira Press.
———. 2013a. *Bali tourism*. London: Routledge.
———. 2013b. *Media, myth, and society*. New York: Palgrave.
———. 2013c. *Theorizing tourism: Analyzing iconic destinations*. Walnut Creek, CA: Left Coast Press.
———. 2019a. *Media analysis techniques*. 5th ed. Thousand Oaks, CA: Sage.
———. 2019b. *Three tropes on trump: A textbook on applied Marxism, semiotics and psychoanalysis*. New York: Peter Lang.
———. 2020a. *Media and communication research methods*. 5th ed. Thousand Oaks, CA: Sage.
———. 2020b. *My name is Sherlock Holmes: Sherlock Holmes is introduced to cultural theory: A didactic mystery/textbook*. Mill Valley, CA: Marin Arts Press.
———. 2020c. *Marx EST mort: Sherlock Holmes is introduced to modern Marxism*. Mill Valley, CA: Marin Arts Press.

Jameson, Fredric. 1991. *Postmodernism or, the cultural logic of late capitalism.* Durham, North Carolina: Duke University Press.
Patai, Raphael. 1972. *Myth and modern man.* Englewood Cliffs, NJ: Prentice-Hall.
Solomon, Jack. 1990. *The signs of our times: The secret meanings of everyday life.* New York, NY: Perennial.

CHAPTER 7

An Ethnographic Case Study: My Everyday Life During the Pandemic

Chapter Objectives This chapter is an ethnographic study of the way the author spent the first 2 years of the pandemic more or less confined to his house. At first, it was because of restrictions put on everyone at the beginning of the pandemic and later, after vaccines were developed and made available to everyone, because he is immunocompromised. It is based on Henri Lefebre's notion that everyday life is based on recurrences. It lists the author's daily routine in considerable detail. When the author taught media criticism at San Francisco State University, he had his students write analyses of various episodes of the British cult series, *The Prisoner*. It was ironic that like Number 6, the hero of the series, he also ended up a prisoner and was held in confinement not by Rover, the killer weather balloon of the series, but by a virus similar in shape to Rover but infinitely smaller.

Keywords Ethnographic • Recurrence • Pandemic • *The Prisoner*

> Thinking consists not of "happenings in the head" (thought happenings there and elsewhere are necessary for it to occur) but of traffic in what has been called, by G. H. Mead and others—significant symbols—words for the most part but also gestures, drawings, musical sounds, mechanical devices like clocks, or natural objects like jewels—anything, in fact, that is disengaged from its mere actuality and used to impose meaning upon experience. From the point of view of any particular individual, such symbols are largely given. He finds them already current in the community in which he is born and they remain, with some additions, subtractions, and partial alterations he may or may not have had a hand in, in circulation when he dies.

> Clifford Geertz, *The Interpretation of Cultures*. New York: Basic Books. 1977.

> Metaphor is for most people a device of the poetic imagination and the rhetorical flourish—a matter of extraordinary rather than ordinary language. Moreover, metaphor is typically viewed as a characteristic of language alone, a matter of words rather than thought or action. For this reason, most people think they can get along perfectly well without metaphor. We have found, on the contrary, that metaphor is pervasive in everyday life, not just in language but in thought and action. Our ordinary conceptual system, in terms of which we both think and act, is fundamentally metaphoric in nature ....The concepts that govern our thought are not just matters of the intellect. They also govern our everyday functioning, down to the most mundane details. Our concepts structure what we perceive, how we get around in the world, and how we relate to other people. Our conceptual system thus plays a central role in defining our everyday realities. If we are right in suggesting that our conceptual system is largely metaphorical, what we experience and what we do every day is very much a matter of metaphor.

> George Lakoff and Mark Johnson, *Metaphors We Live By*. Chicago: University of Chicago Press. 1980.

I've lived in Mill Valley, California, a small town five miles north of the Golden Gate Bridge, since 1970. On March 13, 2020, the governor of California ordered people in northern California to "shelter in place," so since that time, my wife and I have generally stayed home, except for short walks around the neighborhood. Mill Valley is in Marin County, one of the wealthiest counties in California.

Because of the fires raging in California and Oregon, the air quality in Mill Valley at times was terrible and we spent a month staying in our homes and only venturing out to get the newspapers and the mail.

Because I am elderly and am immunocompromised, I've not gone to a store since March 13th so we get all our groceries using Instacart or some other delivery service. I purchased a year's subscription to Instacart never thinking I'd use all 12 months of my subscription. And now, as I write this, I am on my second year's subscription.

There is no way to determine how protected I am so I have to consider myself unprotected because I am immunocompromised and the regular vaccinations don't work for me.

Recurrences

Everyday life is full of recurrences, which are so much part of our lives that we often pay no attention to them. During the pandemic, my life has been reduced to the basics, but in some respects, it isn't that much different, because I am a writer and am used to spending a great deal of time at my computer, writing.

Before the pandemic, my wife and I went to the gym every Monday, Wednesday, and Friday morning for more than 20 years. On Fridays, we went to some grocery stores to get food for the next week. We did a great deal of international travel and took four trips the year before, including a cruise from Santiago, Chile, to Los Angeles, a cruise from San Francisco to Alaska and back, a cruise in the Caribbean for 10 days, and a cruise from Dubai to several countries in the area.

We were set to spend 10 days in Guadalajara in an apartment from March 18 to March 28, 2020, when the virus struck and I had to cancel our visit. My wife and I don't usually take so many cruises and generally visit countries on our own, staying in Airbnb apartments.

We also used to go to restaurants from time to time, but not often since we spent so much time dining "out" on cruise ships. One reason I like to take cruises is I can take a break from cooking. I've also written a book on *Ocean Cruising and Travel* and several other books about cruises we took.

As I said earlier, the pandemic changed our lives in many respects, but not in other ways. If everyday life is based on recurrences, let me list some of them that have been part of my everyday life for the past 2 years.

1. I make a to-do list every evening, in which I also plan the meals for the next day. I do all the cooking for lunch and dinner and decide what we will have (Fig. 7.1).

I use my Instant Pot a great deal. I bought it to make yogurt (you press one button and wait for 8 h) but use it for many other dishes. You can only use the one-button yogurt process with special milk. I buy the milk I use at the Dollar Tree store by the carton. I buy three twelve-quart cartons at a time and it lasts for a few months.

2. Since I do the cooking (and have since 2003, when I retired), I also order the groceries and do that on Instacart every Tuesday afternoon or evening, when the ads appear for the local supermarkets. I use Instacart to purchase food at a supermarket chain called Smart & Final or from Costco and occasionally from other supermarkets.
3. I make my bed every morning. Something I learned to do while in the US Army. I was drafted in 1956 and served until 1958 as a public infor-

Fig. 7.1 Three-quart Instant Pot

mation specialist in Washington D.C. Making my bed means I start every day with a sense of decorum. I also fold all my underwear, something I also learned in the army.

4. I get the newspapers every morning. We read the *Marin Independent Journal,* the *New York Times,* and *The Wall Street Journal.* We get these papers every day they are published. I often find articles in these papers I can use in my writing.

   My wife rants about how she despises Trump every morning when she reads something about him in the newspapers. As a result of her behavior, I wrote a book on Trump, *Three Tropes on Trump,* and another book on his followers, *Trump's Followers,* as a means of exorcizing Trump from my consciousness—to the extent that is possible, of course. I also have written about Trump in various books I've published since my *Trump's Followers* book. Even though he lost the election, he hasn't gone away and is still in the news, all the time. But no longer on Twitter (Fig. 7.2).

5. I have the same breakfast: a bowl of oatmeal, a cup of coffee (my version of a cappuccino), and half a bagel. I often also have a soft-boiled egg. I zap the cereal in our microwave for 3 min. My wife has the same breakfast except most of the time she drinks tea instead of coffee (Fig. 7.3).

   With home-made peach preserves from our peach tree and hot milk.

6. I keep a journal and write in it off and on all day. I record how much I sleep and what the temperature is and write about other matters, including my ideas for this book (Fig. 7.4).
7. I have been keeping a journal since 1954 and have written more than one hundred journals plus twenty or thirty separate travel journals. I take

Fig. 7.2 Three Tropes on Trump

Fig. 7.3 Oatmeal breakfast

notes when we travel because I have written half a dozen travel books about our visits to India, Thailand, Vietnam, and Bali. I also spend some time thinking about new projects (Fig. 7.5).

8. I spend 30 min on our exercycle and watch the news. I also do three sets of vertical pushups and lift five-pound weights. When the air quality is decent, my wife and I walk around the neighborhood for around half an hour. Because of the fires in California, we had many weeks in which we were told not to leave our houses due to the terrible air quality.

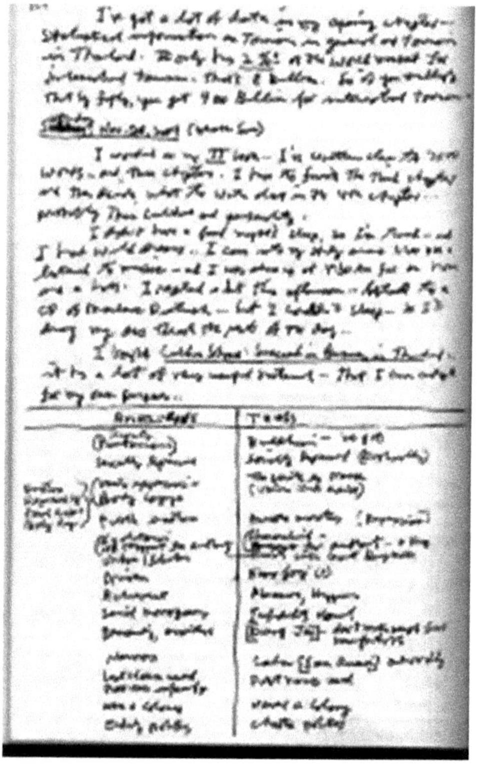

Fig. 7.4 Journal page

9. I go to my computer and work on various projects. I work at the computer, on and off, for a few hours each day. I generally have two or three books in various stages of publication and other projects to occupy my time. For the last 10 years, I've been waking up after 3 or 4 h of sleep, so I go to my computer and write for an hour or two, and then return to bed. So by 7:30 AM or 8:00 AM, when I wake up again, I've already worked for a couple of hours.

    I also spend some time every day deleting the torrent of email messages I get. My life since March 2020 has become essentially "virtual."

10. My wife and I watch about an hour of television most days, though, on occasion, such as when there is a good football game, I watch more. I have written some articles about sports over the years since I see sports as part of popular culture. When I was in the Army, I was a high school sports reporter for the *Washington Post* on weekend evenings. I have written a book, on the semiotics of sport, that has been accepted for publication but I have no idea about when it will be published.

11. I read for a while every evening before I go to sleep. I am currently reading Karen Armstrong's *Jerusalem*, a superb book.

Fig. 7.5 *The Golden Triangle: An Ethno-Semiotic Tour of Present-Day India*

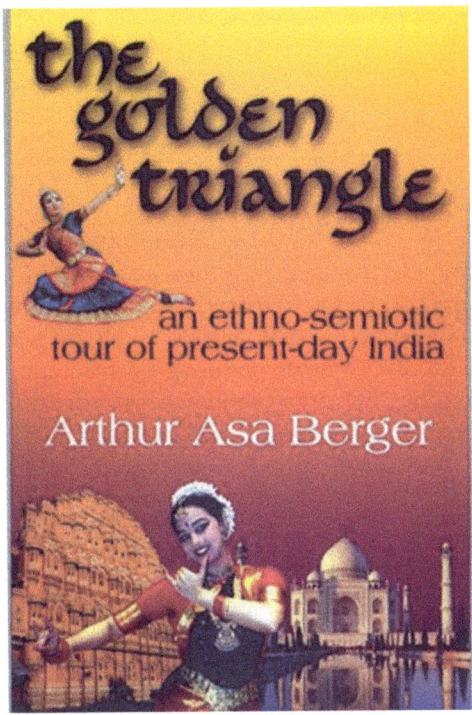

12. I take out the garbage every Thursday. We have three large bins that I roll up our driveway and leave on the road.
13. I order groceries using Instacart to be delivered every Tuesday or, on occasion, Wednesday morning. We can get our groceries delivered in 2 h thanks to Instacart.
14. My wife and I Skype with our son and his family every Friday afternoon and with our daughter and her family every Saturday morning.

An Eventless Life?
My life, in many respects, can be described as eventless. During the pandemic, my everyday life has been reduced to many relatively trivial routine activities due to our social isolation. I often describe my life now as being under "house arrest," and 1 day is so much life the next that like many people, I have trouble keeping track of what day it is. I describe my situation as living a "reduced" life. We used to have season's subscriptions to three theater companies, we went to the gym three times a week, and we took many foreign trips. Our last trip was a cruise that we took from Dubai in 2020.

This has been how my wife and I have been living since March 2020. During this period we've only bought gasoline four or five times, and generally, we only use our car to drive to medical appointments. My wife had an accident and broke her sternum and that has led to numerous visits to hospitals to check up on her progress.

The pandemic has exacerbated the eventlessness of our lives and the lives of most people. Senator William Fulbright said that most people's lives are, when you think about it, minor events on the ongoing universe and our lives are generally only of concern to ourselves, our families, people we work with, and our friends.

In ordinary times, we create events—weddings, birthday parties, dinner parties, meetings, etc. but they are only personally important. But that is enough for most people. Henry David Thoreau wrote that the mass of men lead lives of quiet desperation, but somehow we manage to cope with this by becoming part of consumer cultures, by belonging to organizations of one kind or another, by joining churches, synagogues, or other religious organizations that provide companionship and solace.

The question on my mind, as I write this, is when will we fully escape from the pandemic, the primary cause of the extreme eventlessness in our lives, and of the isolation that is so difficult for us to bear. In ordinary times, everyday life is full of what might be called "escape attempts," in which we find ways to be with others and find things to do of interest. Now that we are all suffering from the pandemic, escape attempts are increasingly important in everyone's lives.

The remarkable speed with which scientists have developed vaccines has changed things for most people, and as I write this, life for many of us is returning to a vague semblance of normalcy. But because wearing masks and getting vaccinated has become politicized, even vaccinated people still are suffering from the impact of the virus and it is questionable whether we will ever escape from it. That is because many people refuse, for one reason or another, to get vaccinated. Sadly, thousands of people are dying who could be saved if they wore masks and were vaccinated. We can see a light at the end of the tunnel, but the tunnel has become much longer because of vaccine hesitancy and resistance.

My life hasn't changed at all since March 13, 2020, except that I've written several books that are in the process of being published. So I spend a good deal of time writing to publishers and interacting with acquisition editors who might be interested in publishing my books.

I've done around a dozen virtual lectures at conferences on media or semiotics since I've been stuck at home. For some reason, I am very popular in India and an advertisement for one of my lectures described, much to my amusement, me as a "living legend." For me, it is the "living" part that is important.

Summary

The pandemic has had a great impact on everyone's lives and has turned many of us into prisoners of our homes where recurrences are evident and where life has a kind of bizarre eventless quality. Each day is like the one before it. The

Fig. 7.6 The Prisoner meets the first Number Two

routines that are part of each day are more evident since there is so little else going on in my life.

I booked a 15-day cruise from San Francisco to Hawaii and back on a Princess ship but had to cancel it. My oncologist said it was too risky.

The Prisoner (Fig. 7.6)

When I taught courses on media criticism at San Francisco State University, I used to have my students analyze episodes of a British show, *The Prisoner*. It starred Patrick McGoohan and had a cult following. It was broadcast in 1966–1967.

The character played by McGoohan resigned from the secret service in England, was gassed, and ended up on an island full of spies who had also been brought to the island. Everyone on the island was given a number.

The Prisoner was Number Six. Each episode he battled with a new Number Two. Number One was never seen. The people who ran the island used a gigantic weather balloon, Rover, to kill people and maintain control over everyone on the island (Fig. 7.7).

It is only poetic justice, I imagine, that I became a prisoner, but it was not Number One or Number Two with whom I had to battle, but a virus. McGoohan escaped from his imprisonment in "The Village" after 17 episodes. When I will escape—if I ever do escape—and be able to lead a normal life remains to be seen. I can only hope that scientists will come up with a vaccine or with pills that will change things for me and everyone else who is immunocompromised. Until then, I don't have Rover to contend with but something very similar, the coronavirus (Fig. 7.8).

Fig. 7.7 Rover, The Killer Balloon, in *The Prisoner*

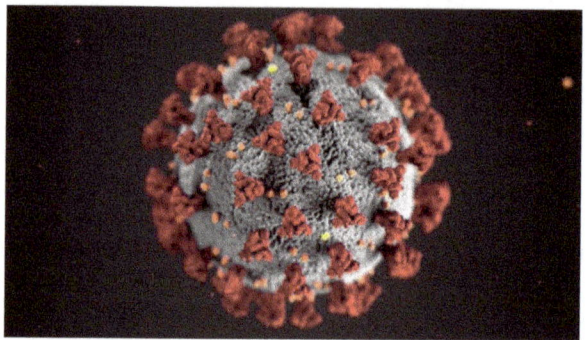

Fig. 7.8 The Coronavirus

Update

In December of 2021, it was announced that Evusheld, a new vaccine for immunocompromised people, has been approved and will soon be made available and pills that prevent the virus from functioning in people who have been affected, if administered during the first 5 days, have been developed, so now I suspect my life and the lives of many people with immunity problems will change radically.

References

Geertz, Clifford. 1977. *The interpretation of cultures.* New York: Basic Books.
Lakoff, George, and Mark Johnson. 1980. *Metaphors we live by.* Chicago, IL: University of Chicago Press.

CHAPTER 8

Coda

Chapter Objectives This chapter is a study of the creative process and the role the author's journals have played in his writings.

It reproduces several pages from his journal to show how he got the idea of writing this book and some of his brainstorming in his journal about the book. It also deals with a topic informing the book, the matter of time spent with media which the author believes "consumes" everyday life, and the impact of social media and digital culture upon our individual lives and society.

Keywords Quotidian • Everyday life • Journals • Digital culture • Postmodernism

> There is a series of phenomena of great importance which cannot possibly be recorded by questioning or computing documents, but have to be observed in their full actuality. Let us call them the imponderabilia of actual life. Here belong such things as the routine of a man's working day, the details of his care of the body, of the manner of taking food and preparing it; the tone of conversational and social life around the village fires, the existence of strong friendships or hostilities…All these facts can and ought to be scientifically formulated and recorded, but it is necessary that this be done, not by a superficial registration of details, as is usually done by untrained observers, but with an effort at penetrating the mental attitude expressed in them.
>
> Bronislaw Malinowski, *Argonauts of the Western Pacific* (1961:18-19):

> Everyday life is made of recurrences: gestures of labour and leisure, mechanical movements both human and properly mechanic, hours, days, weeks, months, years, linear and cyclical repetitions, natural and rational time, etc.
>
> Henri Lefebvre, *Everyday Life in the Modern World* (1971). (Table 8.1)

I have been keeping journals since 1954 and now am on number 104 which I started on January 1, 2021. One day I was writing in one of my journals when, out of the blue, the notion of writing a book, or more precisely another book, on everyday life popped into my head. It would deal with everyday life in the postmodern world and update Henri Lefebvre's classic work *Everyday Life in the Modern World* (1971).

I decided on a title:

Table 8.1 Average time spent per day with major media by US adults

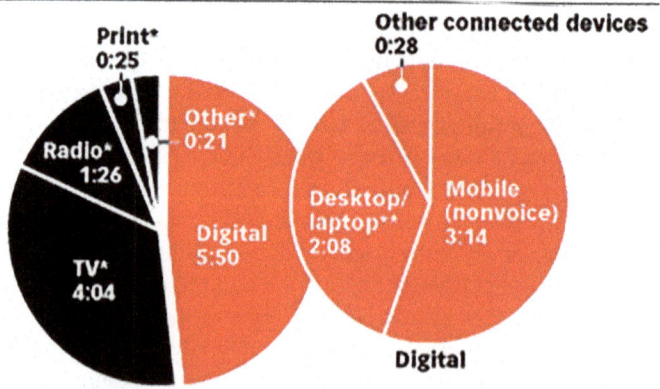

AQ *American Quotidian:*
Everyday Life in the Postmodern World.

So my book would deal with everyday life and with postmodernism, to topics that I've written about many times. I wrote the title in large letters on the page and then divided the rest of the page into four columns and did some brainstorming on the idea. I divided part of the next page into four columns and did more brainstorming, listing topics I might deal with (Fig. 8.1).

The next figure shows the page on which I got the idea of writing a book on everyday life in the postmodern world. Later in my journal, I devoted an entire page to working on the book and I devoted many pages in my journal to the project (Fig. 8.2).

It is fair to say that all of my books have started this way: I get an idea, play around with it here and there in my journal, and when I have a sense of how the book might be structured, I start writing. I do not plan every chapter in detail, like some authors, but launch the book with a general idea of what I want to write about.

If you consider the amount of time the average adult American spends with the media: more than 4 h a day watching television and more than 5 h a day involved with the Internet, plus time with radio and cell phones, you can see that popular culture is much of the content of our everyday lives, so when I wrote my books on popular culture I was really writing about everyday life and when I wrote about everyday life, much of what I wrote about was on popular culture.

Fig. 8.1 Journal page when the idea of writing a book came to me

Fig. 8.2 Journal page: Brainstorming on everyday life

My book, *Pop Culture,* was published in 1973, so I have been writing about pop culture and everyday life for almost 50 years (Fig. 8.3).

I hope that my readers will find this book on the American quotidian and everyday life in the postmodern world interesting and useful. It is full of ideas about all kinds of things relating to our everyday lives in the postmodern world (some would say we now live in a post-postmodern world) and offers insights into our lives and American culture that I think are worth considering and taking seriously. As a result of the pandemic, my life—and the lives of many Americans—became what I describe as "virtual," or tied to Zoom, Skype, our mobile phones, the Internet, and other aspects of our electronic and digital culture.

It seems to me, as I think about postmodern America, we have to consider the role of electronic gadgets and gizmos in our everyday lives. Earlier in the book, I reprinted a table from eMarketer which showed that a few years ago the average adult American spent 12 h and 7 min every day with media:

Fig. 8.3 Cover of *Pop Culture*

4.04 hours with television
5.50 hours with digital devices of one sort or another
1.20 hours with radio
.26 hours with print

I Googled a question on May 30, 2019: how much time does the average person spend with a cell phone and received this answer:

> The average US adult will spend 2 hours, 55 minutes on a smartphone in 2019, a 9-minute increase from 2018. Among smartphone users in the US, time spent with their device is 3 hours, 10 minutes per day.

Those 3 h are part of the 5.50 h we spend with digital devices. Another Google search revealed the following information about how often we check our cell phones:

Americans check their phone on average once every 12 minutes—burying their heads in their phones 80 times a day, according to new research. A study by global tech protection and support company Asurion found that the average person struggles to go little more than 10 minutes without checking their phone.

I read somewhere that many teenagers take their cell phones to bed with them, lest they miss a message, and some send as many as one hundred texts a day to their friends.

Digital Culture and Postmodernism

So to be postmodern in America (and most other countries as well) is to be involved with electronic devices and the digital world for enormous periods of time. We must recognize, also, that our digital experiences have an impact on our psyches and everyday lives.

My point is that our saturation in digital culture in our postmodern society and the digital devices we use have consequences on us and on American culture and society of which many of us are unaware. Consider, for example, the impact of video games. As I explained in my book *Media Analysis Techniques* 5th edition (2019):

> Video games have incredible potential to influence players. Their unique power can be used to teach and entertain people in new ways. Many games require players to heighten their powers of observation, infer rules from their observations, and deal with information from a variety of sources, such as nonverbal cues. Some video games may be described as prosocial and as having positive effects on their players. Unfortunately, however, most video games are similar in nature to the kinds of shows that make up the majority of the programming content on television, which has famously been described as a "vast wasteland." In this respect, video games are no different from other kinds of mass-mediated popular culture.
>
> The function of the media analyst who examines video games is to apply to these texts the various methods of criticism described in this book, to understand how they achieve their effects and what their impacts are—both on those who play the games and on society. I have offered above what might be described as an overview of some of the more interesting aspects of video games. A considerable literature on video games now exists, and an enormous number of Internet sites are devoted to video games in general and to particular video games. Some universities and a number of art schools are now offering degrees in creating video games. Some of the newer video games released in 2010 are so realistic and lifelike that players become disturbed when they play them. A reviewer of Sony's new baseball video game MLB 10 complained that he found it difficult to play and became mildly upset because of the astonishing visual elements found in it.

The video game business is an enormous one. Video game players, known as "gamers," will spend $175 billion on video game software worldwide. In the USA, "gamers" spent more than $33 billion on video game players, accessories, and software, according to an article, "Gaming Industry Thrives Amid Quarantines. Can it Be Sustained?" in the November 13, 2020, *New York Times*.

Many video players become addicted to "gaming" with terrible consequences. I recall reading an article a few years ago about the problems video game addicts cause in Korea, which set up camps to deprogram video game addicts. Finally, we must consider the impact of the Internet on individuals and society. Philosopher Herbert Dreyfus has a perspective on the Internet that focuses on the problems it creates.

In his 2009 book, *On the Internet,* Second Edition, Dreyfus discusses the negative effects of the Internet on people. He argues that people have lost the ability to converse with others because they are so used to one-way communication using email and text messages. He got this idea from Sherry Turkle, a professor at the Massachusetts Institute of Technology who talked about people being "alone together" during an interview on Fresh Air. Dreyfus suggests that social media are not just harmless diversions but have a major impact on our psyches, and not in a positive manner, with many people who use the Internet reporting increases in their loneliness and depression.

I've tried to suggest in this chapter that in various areas the "electronic imperative" that shapes our relationship with media and digital culture, in general, is dangerous to our well-being and American society and culture in many respects. Postmodernism is, among other things, digital and the impact of digital devices and digital culture on us and our societies is enormous.

Writing a book is a labor of love. I've revised, updated, and rewritten this book a dozen times—always looking for the right word in various places in the book and thinking about how my readers will react to my ideas and those of the people quoted in the book. You have to think about every word you use and every idea you deal with when you write, so there is an element of stress involved in writing a book, or writing anything, for that matter.

I started the book with a quotation from Robert Musil's *The Man Without Qualities,* in which he writes about the way life catches up with us and we become like flies covered over by flypaper glue, and I ended the book with a discussion of digital media. I have provided quotations from many wonderful writers and major thinkers all through the book, to amplify some of the topics I wrote about and offer ideas worth taking seriously. If you see the world a bit differently after reading this book and maybe even see yourself differently, I will feel that my efforts have been worthwhile.

References

Berger, Arthur Asa. 2019. *Media analysis techniques.* 5th ed. Thousand Oaks, CA: Sage.
Lefebvre, Henri. 1971. *Everyday life in the modern world.* New York: Harper & Row.

Glossary

Alienation This involves estrangement from the self (from *alien,* which means someone with no connections to others). For Marx, alienation is the central problem of capitalist societies and affects everyone in them; capitalism produces material things, but it also produces alienation.

Amazon Echo Dot This device is a smart speaker that recognizes human speech and can do many things such as act as a timer, play news, play music, answer questions, and so on.

Ambivalence In psychoanalytic theory, a defense mechanism involves a feeling of both love and hatred or attraction to and repulsion toward the same person or thing.

Anomie This is a condition in which people reject the norms of a given society (from the Greek anomos, meaning "no norms" or "no law"). The term was made popular by the French sociologist Émile Durkheim.

Base This involves, in Marxist thought, the economic system found in a given society. Marx argued that the base shapes (but does not determine) the superstructure—the institutions found in the society, such as art, religion, the legal system, and the educational system.

Class or Socio-economic Class A group of people who have something in common; the term refers primarily to social class or, more literally, socioeconomic class—groups of people who differ in terms of income and lifestyle. Marxist theorists argue that there is a ruling class that shapes the ideas of the proletariat, the working class, and generates "false consciousness" to prevent revolution.

Class conflict For Marxists, history is the record of class conflict. This conflict ends when capitalism is replaced by communism and all classes are eliminated because then everyone will own the means of production.

© The Author(s), under exclusive license to Springer Nature Switzerland AG 2022
A. A. Berger, *Everyday Life in the Postmodern World*, Springer Texts in Social Sciences, https://doi.org/10.1007/978-3-031-07926-9

Codes In semiotic theory, codes are systems of symbols, letters, words, sounds, and so on that generate meaning. Language, for example, is a code. It uses combinations of letters that we call words to mean certain things. It is important to recognize that the relation between a word and the thing the word stands for is arbitrary and based on convention.

Critical research This suggests a Marxist approach to the study of media that is essentially ideological, that focuses on the social and political dimensions of the mass media and the ways organizations and others allegedly use them to maintain the status quo rather than to enhance equality.

Cultural Capital This term, used by the French sociologist Pierre Bourdieu, refers to the social assets of a person such as education, intellect, style of speech, and style of dress that are connected to social mobility in stratified societies.

Culture Codes What we call culture can be seen to be made up of countless codes of behavior that young people learn as they grow up in a culture or subculture.

Culture There are hundreds of different definitions of the term culture. It generally is understood to refer to specific ideas, arts, customary beliefs, ways of living, behavior patterns, institutions, and values of a group that are transmitted from generation to generation. When applied to the arts, the term elite culture generally refers to elevated kinds of artworks, such as operas, poetry, classical music, and serious novels.

Defense mechanisms In psychoanalytic theory, this term refers to the methods used by the ego to defend itself against pressures from the id (or impulsive elements in the psyche) and superego elements such as conscience and guilt. Among the more common defense mechanisms are repression (barring unconscious instinctual wishes, memories, and so on from consciousness), regression (returning to earlier stages in one's development), ambivalence (a simultaneous feeling of love and hate toward some person or thing), and rationalization (offering excuses to justify one's actions).

Demographics This term refers to statistical characteristics of people such as race, religion, gender, social class, ethnicity, occupation, place of residence, and age. It differs from psychographics which deals with the psychological qualities of groups.

Deviance Deviants are people who differ from the norm, whether in values and beliefs, or actions. Our attitudes toward various forms of deviance change over time. Many groups that are judged deviant are marginalized—that is, pushed to the margins of society, where they can be ignored or persecuted (or both). But many so-called "deviant" groups eventually become accepted and are integrated into the societies where they are found.

Dysfunctional (also Disfunctional) Anything that contributes to the breakdown or destabilization of an organization or a society.

Ego According to Freudian theory, the ego is the executant of the id and a mediator between the id and the superego. The ego is involved with the perception of reality and the adaptation to reality. If the ego is not able to mediate between pressures from the id and superego, problems arise and people with this problem often develop neuroses.

False consciousness In Marxist theory, false consciousness refers to the mistaken ideas that people have about their class, status, and economic possibilities. These ideas help maintain the status quo and are of great use to the ruling class, which wants to avoid changes in the social structure. For Marx, the ideas of the ruling class are always the ruling ideas in society.

Feminist criticism This refers to a kind of criticism that focuses on the roles of women in society and how women are portrayed in mass-mediated texts of all kinds. Many feminist critics argue that women are generally depicted as sexual objects, as housewives, as weak or helpless or mindless, and so on, and this has negative effects on the socialization of young women and young men, and on society in general.

Functional Something is functional if it contributes to the maintenance of a group or an entity or a society. A functional institution, for example, contributes to the maintenance of society. Compare with dysfunctional.

Functional alternative If something takes the place of something else, we call it a functional alternative. For example, professional football can be seen as a functional alternative to religion and department stores can be seen as functional alternatives to churches.

Gender We use the term gender to refer to the sexual category of an individual—formerly masculine or feminine but now not binary—and the behavioral traits connected with each category. Feminist theorists, such as Judith Butler argue that gender is socially constructed rather than being completely natural and can be considered a kind of performance.

Grid-Group Theory This theory was developed by the social anthropologist Mary Douglas. It argues that modern societies have four "lifestyles" based on the number of prescriptions and the strength of the boundaries to which individuals are subjected. These "lifestyles" are Elitist, Individualist, Egalitarian, and Fatalist and are all in conflict with one another.

Id In Freudian theory, the Id is the element of the psyche that is representative of a person's drives. According to Freud's structural hypothesis about the psyche, it is in constant conflict with the ego. The id is also the source of energy, but it lacks direction, and so the ego must harness and control it. In popular thought, the id is connected with impulse and lust.

Ideology There are many definitions of this term. Generally, it is defined as a logically coherent, integrated explanation of social, economic, and political matters that helps establish the goals and direct the actions of some group or political entity. People act (and vote or don't vote) based on their ideologies, even those who have never articulated or given any thought to them. Marxist critics such as Roland Barthes typically seek to expose what they would describe as the capitalist ideology hidden in works of art, literature, and popular culture.

Image Images can be defined as "a collection of signs and symbols—what we find when we look at a photograph, a film still, a shot of a television screen, a print advertisement, or just about anything" (Berger, Seeing is Believing, 1972). An image may be a mental or a physical representation. Images can have powerful emotional effects on people, and some images have historical significance.

Imprinting This term is used by marketer and psychoanalyst Clotaire Rapaille to describe the process by which young children, up to the age of seven, learn the various codes, beliefs, and practices in the country in which they are born. These imprintings, Rapaille argues, play a role all through their lives.

Latent functions The functions refer to the hidden and unrecognized functions of some activity, entity, or institution. Social scientists contrast these with manifest functions, which are recognized and intended.

Lifestyle We use this term to describe the way people live, including the decisions they make about how to decorate their homes (and where their homes are located), the kinds of cars they drive, the styles of clothes they wear, the kinds of foods they eat and the restaurants they frequent, where they go for vacations, and so on. Lifestyle has become an important matter in postmodern societies.

Manifest functions We use this term to deal with the obvious and intended functions of some activity, entity, or institution. Social scientists contrast these with latent functions, which are hidden and unintended. For example, the manifest function of a person's going to a political rally is to show support for a candidate; the latent function might be for the person to meet others with similar political views or search for sexual partners.

Mass This term can be defined as a large number of people who form the audience for some communication. There is disagreement among scholars about how to understand the mass of people who are reached by mass communication. Some theorists believe the mass is made up of individuals who are heterogeneous, do not know one another, are alienated, and do not have a leader. Others assert that this argument is based not on facts or evidence, but on incorrect theories.

Mass communication In communication theory, this term refers to the transfer of messages, information, texts, and the like from a sender of some kind to a large number of people, a mass audience. This transfer is done through the technologies of the mass media—newspapers, magazines, television programs, films, records, computer networks, CD-ROM, and so on. The sender is often a person in some large media organization, the messages are public, and the audience tends to be large and varied. With social media, things have changed and now individuals can communicate to large numbers of people.

Medium A medium is a means of delivering messages, information, and texts to audiences. There most common way of classifying media is to divide them into print (newspapers, magazines, books, billboards), electronic (radio, television, computers, digital), and photographic (still photography, film, video).

Metaphor A metaphor is a Fig. of speech that conveys meaning by analogy. We must recognize that metaphors are not confined to poetry and literary works; according to linguists, metaphors are the fundamental way we make sense of things and find meaning in the world. They always use a form of the verb "to be." A simile is a weak form of metaphor that uses either like or as in making an analogy.

Metonymy A metonymy conveys information by association (for example, using the name Mercedes Benz to convey that something is expensive or high quality). Metonymy is one of the basic ways people convey information to one another, although we generally are not aware of how often we use associations to get our ideas across. There is a form of metonymy in which the whole represents a part or vice versa. It is called synecdoche (for example, using "the Pentagon" to mean the armed forces).

Modern/modernist Modernism is used to describe the period from approximately the beginning of the 20th century to the 1960s. Modernist artists rejected the traditional narrative structure for simultaneity and montage and explored the paradoxical nature of reality. Some of the most important modernists are T. S. Eliot, Franz Kafka, James Joyce, Pablo Picasso, Henri Matisse, and Eugene Ionesco. Modernism was superseded, according to many culture theorists by postmodernism.

Myths Myths are ancient stories, believed to be true, involving gods and goddesses and heroes that validate our beliefs, customs, and institutions.

Myth Model This model, which I created, suggests that myths can be found in psychoanalytic theory, historical experience, elite culture, popular culture, and everyday life. This suggests that myths play a role in shaping our thinking and behavior, though we generally are not aware of them. I offer examples of the myth model in this book.

National Character Social scientists use the term to describe the basic values and beliefs found in a given country. The Oxford University Dictionary defines it as "the personality or cultural characteristics which are taken to be peculiar to or particularly characteristic of a certain nation or racial group."

Non-functional Sociologists use the term non-functional for something that is neither functional nor dysfunctional. Something that is nonfunctional plays no role in the maintenance or breakdown of the entity in which it is found.

Nonverbal communication Communication that does not involve words, carried out through body language, facial expressions, styles of dress, hairstyles, and so on. Semiotics can shed light on how nonverbal communication works. Poker players are masters at interpreting nonverbal communication.

Pac-Man Pac-Man was a very popular video game that has been around for forty years. The "Pac" stands for Program and Control.

Pastiche Wikipedia defines pastiche as a work of visual art, literature, theatre, or music that imitates the style or character of the work of one or more other artists. Unlike parody, pastiche celebrates, rather than mocks, the work it imitates. It also refers to works that incorporate stylistic elements from other artists or other sources photographs, fragments of advertisements, drawings, pieces of newspapers, etc. According to some theorists, the pastiche is the dominant style in postmodern societies.

Pandemic A pandemic is a widespread disease. The Covid-19 disease is an example of a pandemic, and has been sickening and killing many people everywhere.

Phallic symbol For Freud, a phallic symbol is an object that resembles the penis, either in shape or in function. Examples of phallic symbols are guns, snakes, cigars, and skyscrapers. Symbolism is a defense mechanism of the ego that permits hidden or repressed sexual or aggressive thoughts to be expressed in disguised form. We disguise phallic symbols in our dreams so we are not wakened by our superegos.

Political cultures Political cultures are composed of people who have similar political values and beliefs, based generally on the number of their prescriptions and the strength of their group boundaries. Wildavsky (1989) and his colleagues (e.g., Thompson, Ellis, & Wildavsky, 1990) assert that all democratic societies have four political cultures: Elitists, Individualists, Egalitarians, and Fatalists. and that all four are needed to balance one another.

Popular The means, literally speaking, "of the people" and comes from the Latin term popularis. Popular can be defined in many ways, but it generally is used in the sense of appealing to large numbers of people.

Popular culture We use this term to deal with certain kinds of texts that appeal to large numbers of people. Mass communication theorists often identify (or confuse) popular with mass, and suggest that if something is popular, it must be of poor quality, appealing to the mythical "lowest common denominator." Popular culture is generally held to be the opposite of "elite" culture, which includes arts that require a certain level of sophistication and refinement to appreciate, such as ballet, opera, poetry, and classical music. Postmodernist theorists question this popular culture/elite culture polarity.

Postmodern/postmodernist There is considerable debate about when postmodernism became dominant in American culture. It generally is understood to have superseded the modernist era and started in the 1960s and remained dominant to the present. According to a leading theorist on the subject, Jean-François Lyotard (1984), postmodernism is characterized by "incredulity toward metanarratives" (p.-xxiv). In other words, the old philosophical belief systems that had helped people order their lives and societies are no longer accepted. This has led to a period in which, more or less, anything goes. Postmodern texts may include irony, parody, and the mixing of genres or styles. Some culture theorists argue that we are now in a post-postmodernist era but nobody has found a suitable name for it.

Psychoanalytic theory This theory is based on the notion that the human psyche has three levels and includes an element that Freud calls the "unconscious" whose contents we are unaware of and are ordinarily inaccessible to us (unlike consciousness and the preconscious). The unconscious shapes and affects our mental functioning and behavior. Freud argued that we are all affected by unconscious imperatives, such as sexuality and the role of the Oedipus complex in our lives.

Quotidian The quotidian refers to that which is routine, that happens every day, that is mundane. According to the French sociologist Henri Lefebvre, the quotidian involves recurrence. The opposite of quotidian is remarkable, occasional, or sporadic.

Rationalization In Freudian psychoanalytic thought, rationalization is a defense mechanism of the ego that creates a justification for some action, such as turning in a paper late in a class (or for inaction when an action is expected). Ernest Jones, who introduced the term, used it to describe logical and rational reasons that people give to justify behavior that is caused by unconscious and irrational determinants.

Role Sociologists use the term to describe a socialized way of behaving that is appropriate for a particular situation. We generally play many roles with different people during a given day: parent, student, worker, and so on.

Sacred Sacred means holy and not profane. The sacred–profane dichotomy is a concept posited by the French sociologist Émile Durkheim, who considered it to be the central characteristic of religion: "Religion is a unified system of beliefs and practices relative to sacred things, that is to say, things set apart and forbidden." (Wikipedia).

Semiotics Semiotics, formerly known as semiology, can be described as the science of signs (from the Greek sēmeîon, meaning "sign"). A sign is anything that can be used to stand for anything else. According to C. S. Peirce, one of the founding fathers of the science, a sign "is something which stands to somebody for something in some respect or capacity" (quoted in Zeman, 1977, p.-24). I believe that people are all amateur semioticians since they are always examining others for the messages they are sending through their use of language, facial expressions, body language, and so on.

Social controls We are controlled by the ideas, beliefs, values, and mores in our societies that shape people's beliefs and behaviors. We are both individuals, with certain distinctive physical and emotional characteristics and desires, and, at the same time, members of societies. We are shaped and controlled, to a certain degree, by the institutions—especially education and the media—found in their societies.

Socialization This refers to the processes by which societies teach individuals how to behave: what rules to obey, roles to assume, and values to hold. Socialization used to be a function of the family, educators, clergy, and peers, but the mass media and our digital culture seem to have usurped this function to a considerable degree, with consequences that are not always positive.

Socioeconomic class A group categorized according to income and related social status and lifestyle. In Marxist thought, the ruling class shapes the consciousness of the working class, and history is, in essence, a record of class conflict.

Stereotypes Stereotypes are widely held, simplistic, and inaccurate group-held portraits of categories of people. Stereotypes can be positive, negative, or mixed, but generally, they are negative in nature. Stereotyping always involves gross overgeneralization.

Subculture Within the dominant culture some groups differ in religion, ethnicity, sexual orientation, beliefs, values, behaviors, lifestyles, or in some other way from the dominant culture. Any complex society is likely to have a considerable number of subcultures, and the people in subcultures are often marginalized by those in the dominant culture.

Superego In psychoanalytic theory, the superego is the agency in the psyche that is related to conscience and morality. Freud wrote that the superego is involved with processes such as approval and disapproval of wishes based on whether or not they are moral, critical self-observation, and a sense of guilt over wrongdoing. The functions of the superego are largely unconscious and are opposed to the id element in the psyche. The ego mediates between the two and tries to balance them.

Symbol A symbol is something that stands for something else (from the Greek symballein, which means "to put together"). Symbols bring two things together—for example, a particular object and an act by a character that has some higher meaning. In narratives, certain objects, events, and actions by characters have symbolic significance when they refer to things outside of themselves. Thus in The Maltese Falcon, the falcon has a symbolic significance, representing the villain's greed and obsessiveness and, by implication, the greed of many others—who are willing to lie, cheat, and kill to get their hands on it. The falcon turns out, ironically, to be made of lead, and thus also symbolizes the futility of much human activity and the genius individuals have for acting in self-destructive ways. To understand symbolism, we have to learn (through socialization and enculturation, for example) what various symbols mean.

Text In the context of this volume, any work of art in any medium. Critics use the term text as a convenience, to avoid the need to specify particular kinds of works.

Theory We can understand theory to mean a systematic and logical attempt, expressed in language, to explain and understand something. Theories differ from concepts, which define phenomena that are being studied, and from models, which are abstract, usually graphic, and explicit about what is being studied. Psychoanalysis is a theory. The unconscious is a concept in psychoanalytic theory.

Youth culture Youth cultures are subcultures formed by young people around some area of interest, usually connected with leisure and entertainment, such as rock music or some aspect of computers—games, hacking, and so on. Typically, youth cultures adopt distinctive ways of dressing and develop distinctive ways of behaving.

REFERENCES

Adler, Elkan Nathan. 1930. *Jewish travelers*. London: Routledge.
Adorno, Theodor W. 1948. *Philosophy of modern music*. New York: Seabury.
Bakhtin, Mikhail. 1984. *Rabelais and his world*. Bloomington: Indiana University Press.
Barthes, Roland. 1972. (A. Lavers, Trans.) *Mythologies*. New York, NY: Hill & Wang.
Baudrillard, Jean. 1988. *America*. London: Verso.
Belk, Russel W., Melanie Wllendorf, and John F. Sherry. 1989. The sacred and the profane in consumer behavior: Theodicy and the Odyssey. *Journal of Consumer Behavior.* 16 (1): 1–38.
Berger, Arthur Asa. 1965. McDonald's "Evangelical" Hamburgers. *Minnesota Daily*.
———. 1984. Pac-Man. *Los Angeles Times*.
———. 1997a. *Bloom's morning: Coffee, comforters, and the secret meaning of everyday life*. Boulder, CO: Westview Press.
———. 1997b. *Postmortem for a postmodernist*. Walnut Creek, CA: Altamira Press.
———. 1998. *Perspectives on everyday life: A cross-disciplinary analysis*. New York: Palgrave.
———. 2003. *The portable postmodernist*. Walnut Creek, CA: Altamira Press.
———. 2013a. *Bali tourism*. London: Routledge.
———. 2013b. *Media, myth, and society*. New York: Palgrave.
———. 2013c. *Theorizing tourism: Analyzing iconic destinations*. Walnut Creek, CA: Left Coast Press.
———. 2019. *Three tropes on Trump: A textbook on applied Marxism, semiotics and psychoanalysis*. New York: Peter Lang.
———. 2020a. *My name is Sherlock Holmes: Sherlock Holmes is introduced to cultural theory: A didactic mystery/textbook*. Mill Valley, CA: Marin Arts Press.
———. 2020b. *Marx EST Mort: Sherlock Holmes is introduced to modern Marxism*. Mill Valley, CA: Marin Arts Press.
Berger, John. 1972. *Ways of Seeing*. London: British Broadcasting Corporation and Penguin Books, New York, New York.
Bernstein, Basil. 1972. Social class, language and socialization. In *Language and social context*, ed. Pier Paolo Giglioli. Harmondsworth, UK: Penguin.

Best, Steven, and Douglas Kellner. 1991. *Postmodern theory: Critical interrogations.* New York, NY: Guilford.

Biderman, David. 2010, January 15. Football games have 11 minutes of action. *The Wall Street Journal.*

Bourdieu, Pierre. 1993. *Sociology in question.* London: Sage.

Brenner, Charles. 1974. *An elementary textbook of psychoanalysis.* Garden City, NY: Doubleday.

Brooker, Peter. 1999. *Cultural theory: A glossary.* London: Arnold.

Brooks, David. 2015, September 25. The American idea. *The New York Times.*

Brunskill, David. 2013. Social media, social avatars and the psyche: Is Facebook good for us? *Australian Psychiatry* 21 (6): 527–532.

Chandler, Daniel. 2002. *Semiotics: The basics.* London: Routledge.

Culler, Jonathan. 1986. *Ferdinand de Saussure* (Revised edition). Ithaca, New York: Cornell University Press.

de Certeau, Michel. 1984. *The practice of everyday life.* Berkeley, CA: University of California Press.

de Saussure, Ferdinand. 1966. *Course in general linguistics.* New York, NY: McGraw-Hill.

Denzin, Norman. 1991. *Images of Postmodern Society: Social theory and contemporary cinema.* London: Sage.

Dichter, Ernest. 1960. *The strategy of desire.* Garden City, NY: Doubleday.

Dreyfus, Herbert L. 2009. *On the Internet.* 2nd ed. London: Routledge.

Du Bois, W.E.B. 1994. *The souls of black folk.* New York. NY: Dover Books.

Durkheim, Emile. 1952. *Suicide: A study in sociology* (Trans. J.A. Spaulding and G. Simpson). New York: Free Press.

———. 1965. *The elementary forms of the religious life.* New York, NY: Free Press.

Eco, Umberto. 1976. *A theory of semiotics.* Bloomington: Indiana University Press.

Eliade, Mircea. 1961. *The sacred and the profane: The nature of religion.* New York, NY: Harper & Row.

Engels, Friedrich. 1972. Socialism: Utopian and scientific. In *The Marx-Engels Reader*, ed. R. Tucker. New York: W. W. Norton.

Freud, Sigmund. 1924. *A general introduction to psycho-analysis.* New York: Washington Square Press.

Geertz, Clifford. 1977. *The interpretation of cultures.* New York: Basic Books.

Gerin, Annie. *Devastation and laughter: Satire, power, and culture in the early Soviet State, 1920s-1930s.* Toronto: University of Toronto Press.

Gladwell, Malcolm. 2005. *Blink. The power of thinking without thinking.* New York: Bay Back Books.

Gorer, Geoffrey, and John Rickman. 1962. *The people of Great Russia: A psychological study.* New York: W. W. Norton.

Gottdiener, Mark. 1997. *The theming of America: Dreams, visions, and commercial spaces.* Boulder, CO: Westview.

Hall, Stuart, ed. 1977. *Representation: Cultural representations and signifying practices.* London: Sage.

Haug, Wolfgang. 1986. *Critique of commodity aesthetics: Appearance, sexuality, and advertising in capitalist society.* Minneapolis: University of Minnesota Press.

Henderson, Joseph L. 1968. Ancient myths and modern man. In *Man and his symbols*, ed. Carl G. Jung. Garden City, New York: Doubleday.

hooks, bell. 1992. *Black looks: Race and representation.* Boston: South End Press.

http://culturalstudies.web.unc.edu/resources-2/what-is-cultural-studies/

https://nces.ed.gov/datapoints/2019179.asp
https://www.britannica.com/topic/cultural-studies
https://www.nytimes.com/interactive/2015/10/11/us/
Huizinga, Johan. 1924. *The waning of the middle ages.* Garden City, NY: Anchor.
Illouz, Eva. 1998. The lost innocence of love: Romance as a postmodern condition. *Theory, Culture & Society.* 15: 3–4.
Jameson, Fredric. 1991. *Postmodernism or, the cultural logic of late Capitalism.* Durham, North Carolina: Duke University Press.
Jensen, Joli. 1990. *Redeeming modernity: Contradictions in media criticism.* London: Sage.
Jung, Carl. 1964. *Man and his symbols.* Garden City, NY: Doubleday.
Lakoff, George, and Mark Johnson. 1980. *Metaphors we live by.* Chicago, IL: University of Chicago Press.
Lazere, Donald. 1977. Mass culture, political consciousness, and English studies. *College English* 38: 755–756.
Lefebvre, Henri. 1971. *Everyday life in the modern World.* New York: Harper & Row.
Lenin, Vladimir. 1932. *State and revolution.* New York: International Publishers.
Lyotard, Jean-François. 1984. *The postmodern condition: A report on knowledge.* Minneapolis: University of Minnesota Press.
MacCannell, Dean. 1976. *The tourist: A new theory of the leisure class.* New York: Schocken Books.
Malinowski, Bronislaw. 1961. *Argonauts of the Western Pacific.* New York, NY: E. P. Dutton.
Marx, Karl. 1964a. *Selected writings in sociology and social philosophy* (T.B. Bottomore & M. Rubel, eds. T.B. Bottomore, Transl.). New York: McGraw-Hill.
———. 1964b. *Selected writings in sociology and social philosophy* (Transl. T. B. Bottomore). New York: McGraw-Hill.
Miner, Horace. 1956. Body ritual among the nacirema. *American Anthropologist* 58 (3): 503–507.
Mitchell, Stephen A., and Margaret J. Black. 1996. *Freud and beyond: A history of modern psychoanalytic thought.* New York: Basic Books.
Musil, Robert. 1965. *The man without qualities.* Vol. 1. New York, NY: Capricorn.
Patai, Raphael. 1972. *Myth and modern man.* Englewood Cliffs, NJ: Prentice Hall.
Peirce, C.S. Epigraph. In *A perfusion of signs*, ed. T. Sebeok. Bloomington: Indiana University Press.
Pines, Maya. 1982, October 13. How they know what you mean. *San Francisco Chronicle.*
Poirier, Richard. 1966, May 1. Embattled underground. *The New York Times.*
Pynchon, Thomas. 1965. *The crying of lot 49.* Philadelphia, PA: J. B. Lippincott & Co.
Rapaille, Clotaire. 2006. *The culture code: An ingenious way to understand why people around the world live and buy as they do.* New York, NY: Broadway Books.
Rieff, Philip, ed. 1963. *Freud: Character and culture.* New York, NY: Collier Books.
Simmel, Georg. 1950. *The metropolis and mental life.* Quoted in David Frisby and Mike Featherstone, (eds.) *Simmel on culture.* Page 184. Taken from Hans Gerth (trans.) Kurt H. Wolff (ed.), *The sociology of Georg Simmel,* Glencoe: Free Press, pp. 409–424.
———. 1965. The Poor (Transl. By Claire Jacobson). In *Social Problems, XIII, 2 (Fall).*
Solomon, Jack. 1990. *The signs of our times: The secret meanings of everyday life.* New York, NY: Perennial.

Stevenson, Nick. 1985. *Understanding media cultures: Social theory and mass communication*. London: Sage.

Thompson, Michael, Richard Ellis, and Aaron Wildavsky. 1990. *Cultural theory*. Boulder, CO: Westview.

Wildavsky, Aaron. (1982) *Conditions for a pluralist democracy or cultural pluralism means more than one political culture in a country*. Unpublished manuscript.

Wildavsky, Aaron. 1989. Choosing Preferences By Constructing Institutions: A Cultural Theory of Preference Formation. In A. A.Berger (Ed.), *Political Culture and Public Opinion*. New Brunswick, NJ: Transaction.

Woolf, Virginia. 1924. *Mr. Bennet and Mrs. Brown. Lecture at the meeting of Heretics Club*. Cambridge University, Cambridge, MA.

Zeman, J.J. 1977. Peirce's theory of signs. In *A perfusion of signs*, ed. T.A. Sebeok. Bloomington: Indiana University Press.

GPSR Compliance

The European Union's (EU) General Product Safety Regulation (GPSR) is a set of rules that requires consumer products to be safe and our obligations to ensure this.

If you have any concerns about our products, you can contact us on

ProductSafety@springernature.com

In case Publisher is established outside the EU, the EU authorized representative is:

Springer Nature Customer Service Center GmbH
Europaplatz 3
69115 Heidelberg, Germany

www.ingramcontent.com/pod-product-compliance
Ingram Content Group UK Ltd.
Pitfield, Milton Keynes, MK11 3LW, UK
UKHW022121230426

12048UKWH00010BA/637